LAZY, ANTISOCIAL AND SELFISH?

LAZY, ANTISOCIAL AND SELFISH?

Stories of hope from a new generation

Gavin Calver and Simeon Whiting

MONARCH
BOOKS

Oxford, UK & Grand Rapids, Michigan, USA

First published in the UK in 2009 by Monarch Books
(a publishing imprint of Lion Hudson plc),
Wilkinson House, Jordan Hill Road, Oxford OX2 8DR.
Tel: +44 (0)1865 302750 Fax: +44 (0)1865 302757
Email: monarch@lionhudson.com
www.lionhudson.com

ISBN: 978-1-85424-916-6 (UK)

Distributed by:
Marston Book Services Ltd, PO Box 269, Abingdon, Oxon OX14 4YN

British Library Cataloguing Data
A catalogue record for this book is available from the British Library.

Printed and bound in England by CPI Cox & Wyman.

Contents

Having been started by the American evangelist Billy Graham in 1946, Youth for Christ exists over 60 years later for the same purpose of taking the Good News relevantly to every young person in Britain. As one of the most dynamic Christian organisations, its members serve local churches, go out on the streets, into schools, prisons and communities, and pioneer new and meaningful methods of reaching young people.

God has used YFC to impact the lives of millions throughout Britain. The staff, trainees and volunteers currently reach over 71,000 young people weekly. There are over 65 local centres, from the Isle of Wight to Inverness, as well as thousands of churches linked to the movement. Among other things, YFC invests in future evangelists and youth workers, serves in schools and young offenders' institutes, provides outreach and discipleship resources for church-based youth work, offers residential opportunities, and places a growing emphasis on peer-to-peer evangelism. British Youth for Christ is part of a wider international family operating in over 120 nations worldwide.

For more information about Youth for Christ in Britain, for prayer points or latest news, please visit www.yfc.co.uk.

Acknowledgments

We both wanted to express our sincere appreciation to those who have contributed to this book. Particular thanks must go to our wives, Anne and Jo, for their patience, support and encouragement. We are grateful to many people for their help in this project: Most specifically we would like to thank the many young people we have had the privilege to meet who have shown us that the future of the church is exciting. Thanks as well to those who have supported and loved us in so many ways at our churches: King's Community Church, Stanmore Baptist Church, St. Boniface and Walnut Hill Community Church. We would also like to thank all at Monarch for their tireless support and help in this project. For the support of friends, we are grateful; they have eradicated many mistakes – but those that remain are all ours!

Foreword

I was a teenager in the sixties, an era that has been described as walking down a corridor with doors to rooms on each side. Behind each door were various alluring possibilities involving sex, drugs, alcohol and the wilder side of youth culture. However, for me and most of my friends the doors were either just ajar or firmly closed and we were forbidden to enter them. Modern-day youth too walk down a corridor, but now the doors are wide open and people inside are partying and beckoning them to join them in experimenting with Class A drugs, multiple sexual relationships and binge drinking until comatose – all perceived to be normal and with nothing forbidden.

However, not everything about the sixties and seventies was bad! This era was also one of amazing possibilities. It was a period of unprecedented opportunity for Christian young people to rise to positions of leadership in local churches and parachurch organizations. I was headhunted to lead CARE when I was in my twenties. Others took up senior posts in Christian organisations in their twenties and early thirties. A whole host of new ministries were spawned and led by a vibrant young leadership determined to break the mould, to ensure that the gospel and Christian truth were communicated in culturally relevant ways and to initiate unprecedented social care and action initiatives in Christ's name.

We need to do it again for a new generation and encourage young people to launch out into ministry that resonates with today's post-modern culture. We must do everything possible to support and encourage our spiritual sons and daughters. We who are more experienced must increasingly take risks with our Christian youth who are in their teens, twenties and early thirties, set them free and let them fly in leadership and ministry – and be there to back them with our prayers and support, especially when they make mistakes!

I highly commend Gavin and Simeon for this book and believe it will have a far-reaching influence. How we thank God for the brilliant work of Christian youth and student ministries, individuals and local churches who are there for this generation of teenagers, in the schools, on the estates, in the clubs, in local churches and in the wider community – doing all they can to reach out to vulnerable youth, offering them Jesus and a changed lifestyle. They need our full-hearted support. I am excited to imagine what will be achieved by these young people with a passion for Jesus and a determination to make the gospel known relevantly to the youth of the twenty-first century.

This book is inspirational, challenging, informative and down-to-earth – a timely eye-opener and a must-read for all who have a heart for the youth of our nation.

Lyndon Bowring,
Executive Chairman, CARE

Introduction

'Lazy', 'antisocial', 'selfish': just three of the negative tags attached thoughtlessly to today's teenagers. If you pay enough attention to the media, you could be forgiven for assuming that young people are an irritation and not worthy to be considered part of society. So many people today would have us believe that a gang of thugs, hanging out on a street corner, waiting to cause trouble, are representative of all young people. It's no wonder the situation seems to be becoming worse as well. After all, why would older people do anything other than fear and mistrust young people, if they are constantly being told about how bad they are?

In our increasingly politically correct world, it seems out of order that you can say whatever you like about young people. This directly defies the accepted logic of the day. Why are young people not protected by the same rules which prevent discrimination against every other minority group? We seize upon derogatory terms such as 'chavs' or 'hoodies' and use these to stereotype a large and highly diverse section of society. The British Government are throwing

ASBOs (antisocial behaviour orders) at young people as if they're confetti. TV, radio and newspapers vilify youths in hooded tops as a generation of muggers. Society seems to assume that young people are constantly looking for trouble and the police seem to treat the young as guilty until proven innocent. It is harder than ever to be a young person today.[1]

Unfortunately none of this is particularly new. Generation after generation have been more than happy to declare the bleakness of youth. How regularly the comment rolls off an older person's tongue: 'It was not like that in my day. Kids respected older people then.' But did they? The quote below is from the ancient Greek poet Hesiod in the eighth century BC:

> *I see no hope for the future of our people if they are dependent on the frivolous youth of today, for certainly all youth are reckless beyond words... When I was young, we were taught to be discreet and respectful of elders, but the present youth are exceedingly wise (disrespectful) and impatient of restraint.*

Perhaps it's time we started accepting how hard it is to be young and replaced our criticisms with affirmation. Let's start helping them to have a more positive view of themselves, the world and their futures.

The writer Jane Shilling summed up the current situation wonderfully in an article for *The Times* newspaper:

> *It is a curious view of the world that sees in groups of children (and young people) not a fund of pleasure and hope for the future, but a source of alarm and distress to local communities.*[2]

Why has this happened? As the family unit continues to erode, it is time for us to get behind young people, not to criticize them. We need to rise up and begin to speak with a positive voice about teenagers in order to counteract their negative portrayal in other sections of society.

As two people who have the immense privilege of working with today's teenagers, we find the situation which Jane Shilling highlights to be highly perverse. In our work we so often see so much that contradicts the media's view of young people. Neither of us are naïve enough to believe that some teenagers do not fulfil the negative caricature with aplomb, but these are in a tiny minority. Many more young people are leading their communities into good, not bad. Young people are unhappy to just go along with the *status quo* and want to improve society, not pollute it. Young people provide a positive input and are helping to build a better future for themselves as well as the rest of us.

We want others to join with us in seeing so much good amongst teenagers. That is why we have written this book. Not to paint a falsely positive picture but to bring some semblance of balance. In this book we are telling some of the untold stories. We wanted you to have the chance to hear some incredible stories of young people making a difference. And not just any young people – Christian teenagers. One of the myths of today is that teenagers and Christianity are mutually exclusive. We trust that this book will paint a very different picture. We hope that these stories will challenge you, encourage you and inspire you – sometimes all on the same page!

Our society is not always all that interested in good stories about young people. We wanted to redress the balance, and so here it is: *Lazy, Antisocial and Selfish? Stories of hope from a new generation.*

Chapter 1

Beginning

It all began the way most revolutions begin – with a desire for something better. To be exact, it all began on a Sunday morning in June, after a typical church service. As Becky and Ruth were wandering out of church, Becky was unusually quiet and seemed distracted. All of Ruth's attempts to start a conversation met with either silence or one-word answers. The two girls emerged into the sunshine and headed for the bus stop.

'What's wrong?' Ruth asked gently.

Becky paused before she answered. 'I'm fed up. I'm just fed up with church.'

'What are you fed up about?'

'It's always the same. There's no life in the worship, the preaching is dull, and nothing about it has any relevance at all to how we live for the rest of the week. There's got to be something better than this.'

Ruth nodded. 'I know what you mean. Nobody looks like they actually want to be there, either. And whenever we offer to do something to help out, they say no.'

'Why do we bother?'

Ruth smiled. 'I'm sort of glad you feel this way. It's a relief to find out I'm not alone.'

By now the girls had reached the bus stop. Becky's frustration continued:

'Nobody seems to care about the people who live around here, either. Everyone lives miles away, drives in and out for a Sunday morning, and won't come near the place for the rest of the week. Nobody even talks to the locals. It's like church is a members-only club or something.'

'Yeah,' said Ruth, beginning to get quite animated herself. 'When Steve and Chloe told people they were planning on moving into the area, everyone looked at them like they were crazy. No one in the church seems to understand why anyone would care about the people around here. They just haven't got a clue.'

Ruth and Becky sat together and waited for the bus. Neither of them said any more. Ruth looked around her. There was graffiti. There was litter. There were blocks of council flats. It couldn't exactly be described as a comfortable place to live. But surely God was interested in the people who lived there. And why couldn't church be just as relevant to a kid who lived in a multicultural, inner-city area as it was to someone who was white, middle aged and middle class? The summer sunshine made everything seem unusually bright and peaceful too. This wasn't such a bad place to be. Why was everyone at church so reluctant to have anything to do with the community?

The bus arrived. Becky and Ruth got on and found a seat.

'So what do we do?' asked Becky.

'I think we've got a choice,' Ruth replied. 'Either we give up and go to another church, or we stick around and try to change a few things.'

'We're going to need some help if we're going to change anything.'

'Yeah, we will. Let's talk to some of the others tonight.'

Later on, Becky and Ruth were back at the church for the evening service. They were a few minutes late, and the service had already begun when they arrived. About twenty people were there, which was an average turn-out for a Sunday evening. Most of the people there were their friends – people about their age, in their late teens or early twenties. The service was fairly typical. The worship consisted of old hymns, led by someone playing the piano, and sung with little apparent enthusiasm. The content of the sermon was good, but Ruth and Becky didn't notice because the preacher's delivery was so poor. Combined with the warm evening, the preacher's voice made it difficult to stay awake.

But during the final hymn, Ruth and Becky woke up. Becky was looking forward to talking to some of her friends. She'd feel better for sharing her frustrations with them. Ruth was looking forward to talking to her friends too. She realized she was feeling nervous about telling them what she and Becky had talked about earlier. What if they didn't understand what she meant? Was it possible that only the two of them weren't happy with the way the church was?

As soon as the service finished, Becky and Ruth started rounding their friends up. A few minutes later, ten of them were huddled in a small room at the back of the church, clutching cups of tea. Cameron spoke up:

'Why are we here, then?'

Ruth took a deep breath. 'Me and Becky were talking earlier, and we're just not happy with the way the church is. I mean, we love the people and everything, but the way we do things here just doesn't seem relevant to us.'

'Yeah,' Becky chimed in, 'and we're not doing anything to reach out to the community. It just feels like we've got a holy huddle that meets once a week, and that's it.'

'So we wanted to talk to you guys about it and see what you think,' Ruth went on. 'Cos if it's just the two of us who feel like this, we might as well leave and go to a different church. But if you guys feel the same way... well, we might be able to do something about it.'

There was a pregnant pause. Steve spoke next:

'I'm really glad you said that. Chloe and I haven't been happy with the way the church does things for ages. And we were beginning to think we were on our own.'

'I think you're absolutely right, Ruth,' Russell added. 'The worship and the teaching in the church just don't seem relevant to us. There's the music, for a start. It's just... well... lifeless. There's no passion to it. And as for the teaching – well, can anyone remember what the sermon this evening was about?'

Nobody said anything. Whatever the sermon had been about, it clearly wasn't going to make much difference to how they all lived for the rest of the week.

'I think the worst part is that we never get the chance to do anything,' Cameron complained. 'We could be preaching and leading worship and things like that, but nobody under forty gets to do that stuff. Nobody seems to think we have anything to offer.'

'There's no creativity,' Chloe observed. 'Really there's no creativity in anything the church does.'

There were murmurs of agreement.

'The really frustrating thing is that there's so much good stuff going on when we meet as a youth group,' said Becky. 'I can really feel God with us when we're praying and worshipping. And I know we're all serious about living for God and telling people about him. So, why can't church be like that?'

'You're right,' Will agreed. 'There's got to be something better for the church than what's happening now.'

'So what do we do?' Cameron asked. Everyone looked at each other. Cameron continued, 'If we say anything to the church leaders, will they really listen to us?'

'We could just all leave and go to another church,' Russell suggested.

'That wouldn't solve anything,' Will objected.

There was a pause.

'I think we need to pray about this,' Steve said, finally.

On Thursday morning, Becky was at school. She was ambling through the corridors on the way to a chemistry lesson, when suddenly Ruth appeared next to her.

'I need to talk to you,' Ruth said, purposefully. 'Are you free now?'

Becky hesitated. This sounded like it could be a good excuse to bunk off chemistry, but she'd missed a few lessons this term already, and there was a modular exam coming up in a couple of weeks. 'Er... not really. Can we talk at lunch?'

'That'll have to do, I suppose.' Ruth sounded annoyed.

'This is important, isn't it?'

'Yes!' The look in Ruth's eyes was a little intense.

Becky looked at her watch. She really needed to get to chemistry. 'Well, what's this about? Tell me quickly, and we'll talk more at lunch.'

'Church,' said Ruth forcefully. 'I know what we need to do.'

The rest of the morning dragged on. Becky struggled to concentrate in chemistry, wondering exactly what was on Ruth's mind. She ended up taking in very little of the revision she was supposed to be doing, and she reflected miserably as the bell went for lunch that she might as well have bunked the lesson after all. Ruth had been in the library for a private study period, but she'd spent most of the time doodling on her pad of paper, gazing out of the window, and wondering what Becky would think of what she had to say.

Finally, lunchtime came. Becky made her way to the dining hall as quickly as she could. When she got there, Ruth was waiting for her, sat at a table on her own and playing a fork around a plate of pasta.

'I've been praying about church,' Ruth said, as Becky sat down.

Becky was slightly taken aback by the greeting. 'Right...'

'And God's spoken to me.'

Becky paused. 'Wow. OK...'

'He's told me we've got to make some changes. All those things we talked about the other night, all the things we're frustrated about – we need to be the ones to do something about them. We need to start something new!'

'Yeah...' Becky nodded slowly. 'That sounds like God.'

Ruth went on: 'We need to start a youth congregation.'

'A youth congregation?'

'Yeah. Almost like a church of our own, except we'll still be accountable to the church leaders. So we'll have our own services and we'll do the preaching and worship leading and stuff like that, but we'll still be members of the wider church, and we'll still have the benefit of their wisdom.'

Becky smiled. 'That's a good arrangement. That's clever. Tell me more, then. What's this "youth congregation" going to look like?'

'Right,' Ruth began, 'it'll be like how church is supposed to be, like the church was in Acts. We'll have a service on Sunday nights that's relevant to us and our friends, and young people in the community. But it'll be about more than just one hour on a Sunday. It'll be about reaching out to the community around us, in words and actions. We'll worship God with real passion and creativity, and we'll give young people a chance to use their gifts to serve God. We need to give young people the kind of chances we've never been given – chances to preach and lead worship.' She stopped and looked straight at Becky. 'What do you think?'

'I think... this is brilliant!' Becky exclaimed. 'Scary, but brilliant. It sounds like a big responsibility, but a big opportunity too. And you're sure about this? God wants us to start a youth congregation?'

'Yeah,' said Ruth, definitely, 'I'm certain. And we need to meet on Sunday nights.'

'You think we should take over the evening service?'

'Yup.'

'What do you think the church leaders will have to say about that?'

'Er... I don't know.' Ruth smiled, slightly sheepishly. 'I just know we've got to talk to them.'

'I think we need to talk to the others first.'

'Yeah, of course. If this is going to work, we all have to be behind it. We have to work together on this.'

Gradually, what they were about to do began to sink in for both the girls.

'This is big,' Becky realized. 'We really need to keep praying about this. Let's get a few people together after youth group on Saturday.'

At 9.30 that Saturday night, six people were left sitting in the church hall when the rest of the youth group had gone. Ruth and Becky were joined by Steve, Will, Russell and Cameron. Everyone seemed to be waiting for Ruth to say something. Patiently, she explained the vision for a youth congregation. She made a conscious effort to hold herself back and not race ahead and risk confusing everyone. She was careful to include all the important points: They should be the ones to do something about their frustrations with the church. The new youth congregation should be like how the church in Acts operated. It should be relevant to young people, empower them and let them use their creativity. It should reach out to the community. It should be about real friendships and a whole-week faith.

'... And we need to meet on Sunday nights,' Ruth finished. 'We should replace the evening service.'

There was silence.

'Come on, guys, what do you all think?' Ruth sounded a little exasperated.

'This is fantastic!' Russell beamed. 'Let's do it!'

'Yeah, you're absolutely right,' Will agreed. 'We've got to do something, and this sounds like a great plan.'

Cameron smiled and nodded. 'Let's go for it!'

'Steve, you're not saying anything.' Becky noticed.

Steve hesitated. 'This all sounds brilliant,' he said slowly, 'but how on earth are we going to get the church leaders to agree to this? And we need to realize that this isn't going to be easy. If it all happens, it's going to be a lot of hard work. Are we ready for that?'

'We've got to try,' Will answered.

'Of course we do,' Steve continued. 'It's very

clear that God's spoken to Ruth about this. And we've got to do something about the way things are with the church. We just need to be aware that this could be a long road.'

There was another silence. Everyone looked at each other.

'We need to pray about this,' Cameron said. 'Particularly about how we talk to the church leaders. We need to pray that God gives us favour with our leaders.'

The others nodded and murmured agreement.

'Shall we pray now?' Becky suggested.

The church leadership team were due to meet on the following Tuesday night. Will spoke to Barry and Helen, the pastors, and arranged for the six of them who'd talked and prayed on Sunday to be at the meeting to share their idea. When Tuesday evening came, the six of them found themselves sat in the church hall, on one side of a table, facing the church leaders. Ruth noticed her hands were shaking slightly. Russell wiped the palms of his hands on his trousers, to get rid of the sweat.

Barry started the meeting. 'Well, everyone, as you can see, we've been joined this evening by some of the young people. They've got an idea they want to share with us, so let's talk about that first. Then they can leave us, and we can move on to the boring stuff.' He smiled wryly. 'Now, then' – he turned to Will – 'what was it you wanted to share with us?'

Ruth shared the vision. By this stage, she was quite well practised.

The reaction was mixed. A lot of the comments from the leaders were far more encouraging than Ruth, Becky and the others had expected:

'This sounds so exciting!'

'You're very brave to even consider this.'

Barry was particularly positive. 'I think this is a brilliant idea. And I think it speaks volumes about your faith and your passion for God.'

But there were also some awkward questions to answer:

'Are you saying you want to break away from the church? You'll be taking all the young people away, and we'll never see them again.'

'What about accountability? Who's going to make sure you're leading this properly?'

'So you want money, then. Well, we can't afford to bankroll something like this.'

'Why do you need to take over the evening service? What's wrong with the way it is?'

Ruth and Will did most of the talking between them, and answered the leaders' questions as best they could. They reassured the leaders that they were still very much committed to the wider church, and that the youth congregation would still be very much part of the church as it was. They explained that they meant to be accountable to the leaders for what they were doing, and that they weren't just after money. The discussion took up the next half-hour. At times, it sounded very positive. At other points, objections came up which seemed to put the whole vision in doubt. Finally, Barry called a halt to the discussion.

'I think we've probably said enough. We could probably talk about this all night, but I think we've covered the important points on both sides. In the end, I think this is very simple. If this idea isn't from God, it will fizzle out, and we'll see you back here in a few months, for you to explain what went wrong. But if this is a God idea, one way or another it will happen, and it would therefore be pointless for us to stand in your way.'

Barry paused and glanced at the other leaders before continuing. 'Ruth, this vision of yours is so exciting. We're ready to release you all to do what you think needs to be done. We'll support you, we'll pray for you, we'll advise you... and we might even be able to find some money to make this happen.'

The six friends left the church hall in a daze. They walked out of the church and paused on the pavement outside.

'We did it,' Cameron said softly. The celebrations started. Ruth and Becky squealed and hugged each other. Russell yelled 'Yes!' and jumped on Will. Cameron and Steve just stood and laughed.

'Let's go and get chips!' Becky chirped.

They all realized that there was a lot of work to be done. They all knew that this was risky and there was no guarantee that they'd succeed. But they also knew that God had spoken to them, and that they had to follow where he was leading. And if they wanted things to change, they had to be willing to be the ones to change them.

Six months later, after a lot of serious planning and prayer, the youth congregation met for the first time. The church was packed to the doors with young people. The excitement was tangible. The revolution had begun.

Commentary

I find young people tremendously inspiring. They have a fantastic ability to approach a situation with a fresh viewpoint and real idealism and courage. The true story we have just looked at is a wonderful example of how a group of young people can unite around a cause and pioneer something new and exciting.

There is something about Jesus that makes people instinctively follow him. As he called the first disciples, a group of young people formed around him – the beginnings of a movement that went on to transform the world. It's unlikely that the disciples fully understood what being part of this group would mean, but they chose to unite around Jesus and his cause. In John 1, we read how the disciples caught a glimpse of Jesus, and dropped everything to follow him and do what he was doing. There was no guarantee of success. In fact there wasn't even a guarantee that they were going anywhere specific! They could have had no idea how much following Jesus would transform their lives.[3] But they were still willing to risk everything they had to follow him.

We see a very similar picture with these young people from a modern inner-city church. They caught a glimpse of Jesus and his purposes, and chose to follow him. They gave up a comfortable, middle-class lifestyle and chose to commit themselves to a deprived, needy community. They risked being ridiculed, they risked being misunderstood and they risked failure. As with the first disciples, they had no guarantee of success. But they still chose to follow Jesus and unite around his cause. And this was the beginning of a movement that may not have transformed the world, but has certainly transformed a community.

The first thing the disciples did was to find other people and involve them in following Jesus. Andrew found Simon Peter (John 1:41–42). Philip found Nathanael (John 1:45–46). Excited about following Jesus and his purposes, they couldn't help but invite people around them to be a part of it.[4] Ruth and Becky responded in the same way, encouraging their friends to be part of Jesus' purposes for their church.

A number of the church leaders couldn't

understand what the young people in their church were doing, or why they needed to do it. Perhaps people close to the first disciples thought the same way. Jesus chose surprising people. Why the kids, rather than people with more life experience? Why fishermen, rather than experts in the Jewish scriptures? Why people who'd been rejected by other rabbis? When the church leaders were confronted by six young people, with no experience of church leadership, asking to be released to start a youth congregation, maybe it's understandable that they were hesitant. But they were still humble enough to believe that God could work through inexperienced, idealistic young people. We shouldn't be surprised when Jesus calls young people, and calls them to do new, unusual and risky things. If we're able to help a group of people form and follow a vision from Jesus, we shouldn't be afraid to do so, even if it looks risky.

Think about ...

- Has God given you a vision for something?
- What makes you hesitate about starting something new?
- What would you try to achieve if you knew it was impossible for you to fail?

Chapter 2

Decision

As the minibus rolled into the familiar surroundings of the sterile showground, the four teenage lads turned and faced one another, their blank expressions saying, 'Here we go again, then.'

Year on year, for as long as any of them dared to remember, they had been coming to this same conference. Now that they were fifteen, certain of their maturity and confidently independent, they felt they had outgrown this annual trip. 'Surely we should be at Glastonbury instead,' one of them piped up.

When they were younger, this annual week of camping in a field had been one of the highlights of their year. They could feel like grown-ups, ploughing ahead independently of their parents, if only for a week. They made their own decisions, cooked their own instant meals and were masters of all they surveyed.

Within this week of freedom there had previously been much to enjoy: big bands each night, lots of girls to check out, plenty of football to be played and a good dose of mischief to be had. Previously, the only problem they had encountered was all the Christian rubbish – all that singing and praying, having to listen to some old guy prattle on about some boring and outdated part of that wretched Bible they just wouldn't give up on. However, over years of practice they had mastered the art of zoning out at precisely the right moment – their clever survival mechanism in order to avoid all that religious rubbish. They had always treated this conference like a huge worldly adventure, a theme park where they dictated their day's content, how they behaved and how they responded. For them it certainly wasn't the great Christian festival so many others found it to be. This was and always had been their playground.

Those days were gone and this year things seemed different. The excitement of previous years had evaporated, replaced with a sense of deep monotony. As the minibus driver yanked up the handbrake and turned off the engine, they knew that this year would be completely different. Their enthusiasm had waned and they were only really on site to keep their mums quiet. Before leaving the minibus, the lads made a pact not to go to any meetings, determined instead to derive whatever hedonistic pleasures were on offer to four lads away from home. Jimmy was the leader of the bunch. He was the biggest, the toughest and the mouthiest. He always made sure that the other three – Tom, Jordan and Dave – stuck faithfully to the plan. He was not going to stand for Jordan going soft on them again and sneaking into all those stupid meetings.

As the week progressed, the four of them were pleasantly surprised at how good a time they were actually having. In contrast to the incessant rain of most other years, this time it was unbroken sunshine. The weather was so amazing that you could be forgiven for thinking you were on a desert island, not a British showground! There was a different mood around the place. The week was turning out to be one great big jolly and the boys were particularly pleased to find so many other kindred spirits. These other folks weren't going to meetings either. They too were simply out for having a good time. They were instrumental in forming a large and intimidating posse of teenagers, with Jimmy inevitably leading them all in his well-drilled, autocratic fashion. The gang took great pleasure in having the detached youth team follow them to every corner of this vast showground. It became a sport to them, a game of cat and mouse that took them to every part of the site. No matter how far they went, the intensely keen detached team pursued them zealously.

With the boys having fun and spending money like it was going out of fashion, things soon took a turn for the worse. Somewhat inevitably, by night four of seven, wallets were empty. Suddenly, they were at a loss as to what to do next. Now everything seemed to have a cost attached to it. To make matters worse, they were starving hungry and had already eaten all of their food. What on earth were they going to do next? Determined to make something happen, they walked along aimlessly for a while, trying at least to think of something to help them enjoy the rest of this week. They thought long and hard but came up with no realistic solution. They were broke, bored and beaten.

As they pounded the showground, Jordan spotted the Vicar, Bob, from the church that their parents attended. He was over by the fish-and-chip van. Jordan pointed Bob out and the four lads all drooled at once as they watched Bob tucking into a nice hot portion of chips, covered in tomato ketchup. 'What I wouldn't do for some chips,' they all thought. Dave immediately hatched a plan and told the others that they should get this Vicar to buy them all fish and chips. After all, the Vicar would want to help them, wouldn't he? 'That's what churchy people do, isn't it?' Dave said as Jimmy purposefully led the four of them over towards Bob.

'Vicar, can you buy us some chips? We ain't got no money.' Before Bob could answer, Tom squeakily inserted a 'please'.

Bob had a glint in his eye as he clearly schemed to counteract their plan with an even more cunning one of his own. 'I tell you what, guys,' he said. 'If you go to tonight's youth meeting and sit through the whole thing, then I'll buy you all fish and chips. OK? But the deal is, you have to go to the whole meeting.'

The four lads exchanged glances. What was the next step? An offer of dinner was hard to refuse.

They hated the meetings but right now they felt famished. Surely they should accept this offer and ride out the meeting. But could they really face going to another dull meeting? With hunger overriding their deep-rooted reluctance, they took Bob up on his offer. After all, these meetings only went on for an hour or so, and they could manage that, couldn't they?

The boys tucked into their fish and chips, savouring every mouthful. As grease ran down their chins, their taste buds felt electrified and they felt life spreading through their bodies. Everything seemed good with the world. They finished their meal and, feeling like kings, left to do battle with what they thought lay ahead. However, their triumphant mood was brought to an abrupt end as the reality of the deal they had struck with Bob suddenly dawned on them. Yes, they had enjoyed a free feed, but now they would have to go to this youth meeting. As they looked at Bob, his Cheshire-cat grin said it all. He knew what they were going to encounter, and all in just over an hour's time.

Bob took great delight in escorting them to the marquee where the youth meetings took place. After all, he was going to make sure they fulfilled their part of the bargain. He'd paid out for four portions of fish and chips! The lads entered the meeting moaning about having to sit on the floor, whilst actually secretly enjoying the high-octane games and activities. It got a bit rubbish when the singing started. I mean, who wants to sing songs and dance around when you could be outside in the sun? Still, the memory of those fish and chips lingered on enough to see them through the music.

Then, a young guy jumped onto the stage, grabbed the microphone, and started to talk.

'Who's he?' asked Tom. 'He's not old enough to be a Vicar yet.'

The speaker asked the crowd a rhetorical question: 'What do you want from God?'

Jimmy shouted back, 'Nothing.'

With a wry smile, the speaker decided to take Jimmy on. The other three just looked on with a mixture of sheer incredulity and embarrassment.

'Do you want to come up and share something with everyone?' the speaker asked Jimmy, who now realized he had a few hundred of his peers all staring at him. As Jimmy began to blush, he suddenly wished that he could be anywhere in the world except sitting embarrassed in a huge tent full of people. He decided it would have been better to be hungry again, and to have never laid eyes on Bob. The other three just stared at Jimmy in disbelief. Their leader was lost for words! This wasn't what happened. The silence, which seemed to last for hours, was finally broken when the speaker added a firm and confident, 'Well, be quiet, then, and I won't talk for very long.'

The four of them sat in bewildered silence as the speaker went on to speak about the Feeding of the Five Thousand in John chapter 6. He spoke passionately about this guy Jesus being the God to follow, the God to serve and the God to live for. This speaker was different from what these lads had expected and far from the style of preaching they'd become so accustomed to and resentful of during all their previous church meetings. He was funny, engaging and – surprisingly – didn't have grey hair!

As he shared stories and told the crowd what Jesus had done for them, Tom, Dave, Jordan and Jimmy each felt like he was chatting one-on-one with them. The communication was arresting, the words meaningful, stirring something inside each of them; something in their heart of hearts that told them this speaker was talking truth. Yet there was something more to it. He wasn't just chatting – there was a genuine and tangible sense of the presence of God. Like a bolt from the blue, the truth hit all four of them. This Christian stuff was real after all!

Once he had finished speaking, the preacher got everyone to shut their eyes. He then challenged the crowd that if they wanted to surrender their lives to Jesus, then they should stand, as a sign to God. All four of these lads leapt to their feet at once. Something had changed. It was time for all of them to start living differently.

That night they didn't know what to do with themselves. They were bursting with joy. Exploding with passion, they were desperate to find Bob again.

'Where do you think he is?' asked Jimmy. Impatiently, frantically, they trawled the showground looking for Bob. Finally they spotted him in the distance. They sprinted towards him, and face-to-face with the man who had bothered to buy them dinner, they simply said in loud unison, 'Thank you.'

'For what?' Bob questioned.

Tom replied, 'We went to that meeting you told us about and we've all just surrendered our lives to Jesus.'

Jimmy spoke up: 'We want our friends to become Christians too, so we wondered if you would invite the speaker to come to our church and preach to our friends as well.'

Frankly, Bob had no choice, and he knew that the next morning he would have to find this speaker and land a date. That night Bob, the four lads and many others from the church stayed up till 2 a.m. celebrating what God had done.

Once they got home, the four lads couldn't help but share their faith with their friends. They set up a Christian Union in their school to encourage their Christians peers, and came up with one endeavour after another in the attempt to reach their friends for Jesus: football tournaments, barbecues, music gigs, cooked breakfasts, Youth Alpha – the list went on. They were on fire for Jesus and now found themselves competing with each other for the most entrepreneurial evangelistic idea. All of this was in preparation for the big Sunday event when the speaker they had heard and found so challenging that night in the summer would finally come to their town.

Time seemed to drag unbearably, but eventually the week of the speaker's visit arrived. The lads got every Christian they knew, young and old, praying for the weekend, that God would do great things in the lives of their mates. They went around all their friendship groups and peers, giving out flyers for the event and attempting to drum up as much support as possible. They were determined that no one should miss out.

Sunday finally came around. As the four lads gathered in the church hall to pray with Bob, there was a cocktail of excitement, anxiety and expectation. As Tom was praying, the speaker came walking through the door. It was great to see him again, the four lads thought. Once they had finished praying, they all sat together on the front row, longing for others to join them in the church building. The service began and the normal church attendees were there, but sadly, none of their friends.

'We've really messed up this time,' Dave muttered to his mates. 'The speaker is here, but where's everyone else?' Once the time of sung worship came to an end, Jordan timidly looked over his shoulder at the congregation – more in nervous hope now than confident expectation. He was stunned by what he saw. Half of their year group had actually turned up!

He nudged each of his three contemporaries, who in turn were blown away by what had happened.

It was time for the speaker to take to the stage. The four lads had such a high view of the speaker that they expected something almost mystical to happen as he stood at the front. They were salivating with expectation of a repeat of that night in the marquee. As time went by, they became more disappointed. His humorous style didn't seem the same in this church building on a freezing-cold February morning as it had been back then in the middle of summer. Dressed in a suit, he didn't seem as 'down with the kids' as in his shorts and T-shirt. The talk was OK, but it was nothing like what the boys had hoped for. They were sure that the next day at school they would be ribbed for what they had invited so many of their mates to. They would have to meet together early the next morning to plan their verbal self-defence. The best they could hope for was that in a couple of weeks' time, the whole thing would have blown over.

It was clear that the speaker was now drawing to a close. As he did so, the lads hoped he would avoid asking for a response from the crowd. They didn't want to be embarrassed any further. He did ask. The damage was done now. To their dismay, the speaker asked if anyone wanted to surrender their lives to Jesus. If they did, then they needed to stand. The four lads sat in a row all hunched over, pleading with the ground to swallow them up so they could avoid the embarrassment of hearing their mates get up and leave. Jimmy didn't dare look behind him. Jordan had his head buried in his hands, pretending to pray. Dave was the first one to be brave enough to look up. As he peeked nervously over his shoulder, he was stunned to see at least thirty of his friends standing up and showing that they wanted to follow Jesus. One by one the four lads gazed in amazement at their peers, who like them, had now made this incredible step of faith.

The next day at school, the Christian Union had risen in number from just shy of twenty guys to over fifty. Things at the school would never be the same. Each of these lads was committed to evangelism, desperate to tell all of their friends about the God who had changed their lives. Bob went in to lead the Christian Union one week and asked one of these new converts why it was that they were all so passionate to share their faith with their friends. The reply was simple: 'It's what Christians do, isn't it?'

Commentary

In a number of churches today evangelism has become quite a vague concept. Many are all too happy and willing to do nice things for people – random acts of kindness, social action and generally 'good' deeds – yet it remains fundamental to the faith that we also tell people why we do these things. Jesus told his disciples, 'Whatever you did for one of the least of these brothers of mine, you did for me' (Matthew 25:40), but he also specifically instructed that we should 'Go into all the world and preach the good news to all creation' (Mark 16:15). Word and deed provide a context for each other. Just one alone can never be good enough. It is essential that we Christians share with others the great message of hope that we ourselves have chosen to embrace and live out. And we do this in our action and communication.

When Jesus meets the woman at the well in John chapter 4, it is an incredible encounter. It is in vulnerability that Jesus meets her, not superiority. He is thirsty! With a simple request, 'Will you give me a drink?' (verse 7), a whole dialogue then takes place, in which Jesus speaks specifically into her life, and – despite throwing in the odd cultural and theological curveball to sidetrack Jesus from probing into her life any further – she finally has to acknowledge that this thirsty guy sitting on the side of the well is indeed the Messiah. Jesus doesn't actually get his drink in the end, yet the woman is given living water.

Having encountered the King of the World, something extraordinary takes place in this woman's life. Culturally, she would have been deemed and treated by her community as the lowest of the low. Morally dubious, with a questionable marital arrangement, she was also unfortunate enough to be a woman. In those days the testimony of a woman would not even be heard in court. The average Pharisee got up every morning and thanked God that he had not been born a Gentile, a slave or a woman. No one would have listened to this woman. She had come to the well in the heat of the day in order to avoid the scorn of everyone else. Yet she was not alone. Here she met Jesus.

After encountering him, she rushed back to her village and shared the message with everyone else. Though her testimony would culturally count for nothing, there was something so dramatic, infectious and different about what had happened to her that the whole village ditched their dignity and avoided taking the usual path out of the village, instead rushing across fields in the shortest possible time, in order to get to this Jesus for themselves. In his *Bible Speaks Today* commentary on the Gospel of John, Bruce Milne points out that, 'Having experienced the inclusive love of Jesus for them despite their disadvantages, it was not a difficult step for the Samaritans to arrive at the conviction that this same love was big enough, wide enough and undiscriminating enough to embrace the whole world.'[5] Each of these Samaritans would continue to then share this great message with all of those around them.

Just as it was for the Samaritan woman and our four lads with their fish and chips, when we meet Jesus, we must share him. This revolutionary, life-changing message demands to be shared with all people. We are forever hearing that young people are not interested in Christianity and have dismissed it. Yet the experiences of so many seem to counteract this generalization. There's a great video clip out there of a thirteen-year-old girl sat in a graveyard, explaining why people of her age don't go to church. Her closing comment is arresting: 'It's not that my generation have rejected Jesus – just that nobody has bothered telling us.' We must be faithful and tell people about Jesus, and then let go and trust him to change their lives. A couple of years on, the boys' Christian Union now has over a hundred people attending every week!

Think about …

- How do you feel about sharing your faith with other people?
- Do you find the example of the four lads exciting and encouraging, or daunting and scary?
- Who do you need/want to tell about Jesus?

Chapter 3

Action

The bus growled and shuddered its way through the narrow streets. Sitting on the back seat with four of her friends, Molly took in the scene. The seats in the bus had been mostly removed, and replaced with fold-away tables and chairs, video-game consoles, a sound system and boxes of board games. In the cabinet under Molly's feet was a petrol-fuelled generator. As the bus turned into the High Street, Molly was also uncomfortably aware that the vehicle was painted bright pink. They drew some curious looks from passers-by as the bus crawled through the traffic towards the council estate half a mile away.

It started to sink in for Molly exactly what she was doing. She was part of a small posse of people who were going to park a bright pink bus on a council estate for two hours, open the doors, and invite the local kids, most of whom would be about her age, to come in and play Playstation. When Nathan and Joel, her youth group leaders, had talked about serving people in the community in the name of Jesus, it had sounded like such a good idea. What could be more powerful than doing something practical to show someone that God cared about them? But back then, Molly hadn't realized there would be a pink double-decker bus involved.

She felt the beginnings of a knot in her stomach as she imagined how the residents of the estate would react to a bunch of middle-class teenagers turning up on their doorstep unannounced. Would they be suspicious of them? Would the kids they were trying to reach just run amok and tear the bus apart? Would they just look the other way and completely ignore them?

Serving people was definitely a good idea, but Molly was starting to realize that the experience of actually taking action was fairly uncomfortable. The bus turned ponderously into a side road, pulled up opposite a grimy block of flats and spluttered to a halt.

'Come on, then,' called Dave the driver cheerfully. 'Let's fire up the generator.'

The doors hissed open. Molly found the palms of her hands getting damp with sweat. 'Here we go...' she muttered to herself.

In another part of the town, a small knot of grubby teenagers and an equally dishevelled man in his twenties were trudging along a residential road, going from house to house.

'Please God, don't let anyone be home,' Gary prayed silently as he rang another doorbell. 'I just can't face digging another garden.'

Gary's face and arms were streaked with dirt and dried sweat. His jeans and trainers were caked with mud from three long days of hard work. The tools the group were carrying, which only a few days before had been new, shiny and sharp, had quickly become blunt and misshapen. Gary noticed that his friends all looked as tired as he felt. Even Nathan's encouraging smile was wearing thin. Perhaps Nathan was remembering the rather unnerving experience of the first garden the group had worked on. The owner of the house, a huge man who seemed as wide across the shoulders as he was tall, had looked at the six of them eagerly standing on his doorstep, and wordlessly handed them two brutally sharp machetes. At this, the colour had drained from Nathan's face, and he'd started muttering about risk assessments. The memory of it brought a slow smile to Gary's face as he waited for the door to be answered.

It wasn't that helping people was a bad idea, Gary reflected. He was convinced that God loved to meet people's everyday needs, and it was great to show people that by doing something really practical. In fact, for the first day or two, Gary had really enjoyed himself. There was something really satisfying about looking at a freshly clear and tidy garden at the end of a day's work, and knowing that what you had done had made a difference to someone. The problem was very simple really. It just hadn't occurred to Gary that helping people could be such hard work. How was he supposed to keep going when every muscle in his body was begging for a rest?

There was no answer at the door. Gary silently breathed a sigh of relief.

'Nobody home,' he announced to his friends. The group picked up their tools and moved on to the house next door.

Calvin was excited. He loved football. He loved anything to do with football. He was a quietly spoken type, but he came to life whenever he had a ball at his feet. So Calvin was positively salivating at the prospect of a five-a-side tournament. And they called this 'mission'?! Every time Calvin had heard the word 'mission' before, it had brought to mind either living in a mud hut somewhere in Africa, or handing out tracts in the High Street. Mission was supposed to be hard work, wasn't it? And football wasn't hard work. Football was fun. So how could football be mission?

The teams were picked and a list of fixtures were hastily drawn up. Calvin's team included two of his friends from church and two guys from the estate, who he vaguely recognized as being in the year below him at school. They were scheduled to play in the second match, so Calvin went and sat on the wall at the side of the pitch before the first game kicked off. The pitch was nothing special: just a patch of tarmac, about thirty yards square, with a set of goalposts at each end. There was barbed wire at the top of the fence which surrounded the pitch, and a few shards of broken glass on the tarmac. But Calvin didn't notice how poor the pitch was. He couldn't wait to get playing.

Calvin soon got his chance. The ball zipped across the hard surface as the older, stronger players knocked short, quick passes between themselves. Calvin tried to compromise between playing to win and involving the weaker players in his team in the game. It just about worked. The two younger players in his team weren't very good, but they seemed to grow in confidence as Calvin passed to them more often. They were losing 2–1 with just a few seconds left, but Calvin scored an equalizer with a thumping volley just before the final whistle.

The whole team went back and sat on the wall. Calvin chatted to his younger team mates. He wanted to encourage them about the way they were playing. He'd never spoken to them before, but they seemed friendly, and soon the whole team were chatting and joking around.

'Maybe this is what the "mission" thing is all about,' Calvin pondered. Maybe mission is all about people who follow Jesus, and people who don't follow Jesus yet, getting to know each other and trust each other. Maybe mission is about offering some hope and encouragement to people who wouldn't otherwise have it. After all, everyone needs hope. Calvin wondered when his young team mates had last been told they were good at something.

Looking around him, Calvin began to understand why the tournament was so important. He could see his well-off, middle-class friends from church playing and talking with teenagers from a deprived inner-city estate. And they were playing and talking as equals. The people from the estate were getting the message, loud and clear, that they mattered, that they had talent, and that what they thought counted for something. They were being given hope.

Calvin realized that he'd love to talk to his team mates about God. Maybe that wasn't going to happen today (after all, this was the first time he'd even spoken to them), but one day soon. Calvin smiled. Football, friends and hope. This was his kind of mission. He wondered whether he could do this kind of thing more often. In the meantime, his team were on for their next game.

Gary leaned on his spade as Laura rang yet another doorbell. He started daydreaming about what he was going to do when he got home later. A shower. No, a bath. Definitely a bath. A long one. With a guitar magazine and a big, steaming mug of tea. Gary came back to reality with a start as the door swung open next to him.

'Oh! Hello!' Laura said, with a mixture of surprise and nervousness.

'Hello,' the woman in the doorway replied uncertainly. Her eyes seemed to narrow slightly as she took in the scene on her doorstep. The young amateur gardeners looked at each other self-consciously. Under the gaze of the diminutive woman, they saw themselves as they assumed she must see them: a gang of dirty, sweaty, scruffy teenagers with an assortment of worn-out spades and forks. Gary spoke up:

'Do you need any help with your garden?' he asked. He decided they might as well get this over with.

'My garden?' the small but fierce-looking woman echoed.

'Er... yeah,' Gary nodded weakly.

Without warning, the woman's face creased and tears came to her eyes. Gary felt even more awkward than when she was just looking at him. The woman clasped her hands together and started laughing, even while the tears were running down her face.

'Incredible!' she exclaimed. 'God has sent his angels to help me!'

Gary looked at his friends again. Was she serious? He wasn't sure he'd ever seen a group of people who looked less angelic. They were shabbily dressed, covered in mud and grime, and getting hotter and sweatier by the minute as the summer sun beat down on them.

'Come and see!' the woman beamed, and led them enthusiastically down the passage next to her house and into her garden. Now Gary understood why she was so glad to see them. The garden was an absolute jungle. The brambles and nettles were chest high in places, and there were discarded drink bottles, crisp packets and plastic bags everywhere.

'It was like this when I moved in,' the woman continued, 'and I just don't know where to start. I was starting to think I'd have to pay to have it all cleared, but it'd cost hundreds, and there's no way I could afford that.' She looked Gary straight in the eye. 'It can only be God who's sent you. Your timing is unbelievable.'

Gary smiled back at her. This might just be another afternoon digging a garden to him, but it was clear that this really was a big deal to her. It was just a couple of hours' work, and then it was over for him – he could go home for his bath and his mug of tea. But it was something major for the woman who lived here. They'd save her a pile of money, and more importantly, they'd already shown her that God hadn't forgotten about her.

Gary was tired, but he threw himself into tackling this garden with a new-found energy. This was what it was about, he thought. This stuff really did make a difference. God really did work through ordinary people.

'And please have a go at getting that tree-stump out,' the woman called as she retreated back into the house. 'It's a bit of a job, but just do the best you can.'

The six of them set about their task with relish. To their surprise, two hours flew by as they pulled up weeds, sang raucously, collected rubbish and hacked at the nettles and brambles. Nathan had to look away as Gary attacked the tree-stump with an axe. Gary thought he heard him mumble the words, 'health and safety nightmare'.

The bus soon attracted attention from the residents of the estate. The team were still firing up the generator and setting up the games consoles when two faces peered through the open doors. The two boys were both about nine or ten, sporting tracksuits and extremely short haircuts.

'What's this, then?' one of them asked, sounding confrontational, but just feeling baffled by the pink bus outside his flat.

'It's a bus,' Molly replied, without thinking. Then, realizing what a daft thing that was to say, she went on: 'It's kind of like a youth club on wheels. We've got games consoles, a stereo, loads of other stuff to do. Do you want to come in?'

The boys looked at each other and nodded. 'Yeah, all right.'

That was much easier than Molly had expected.

Within a few minutes, a steady stream of teenagers and younger kids made their way to the bus and wandered in. Older residents came to see what was going on and chat to Dave the driver. Soon, the bus was heaving with young people playing on the games consoles, playing Connect 4 and snakes and ladders, and just chatting to each other and to the team.

The team found they had to be on their toes to make their visitors feel welcome, and also to make sure the equipment didn't get damaged. The two boys who'd come in first just seemed to want to sit and punch each other. A few of the visitors tried to monopolize the games consoles, and needed some encouragement to let other people have a go. A small group of girls who'd been playing Connect 4 soon got bored and decided to throw the pieces at each other instead. And at one moment, the lights went out, the games consoles suddenly turned off, and the stereo fell silent.

'Who switched off the generator?!' Dave shouted. 'You must never touch the generator! It's dangerous!'

It wasn't that these guys were troublemakers, Molly thought. They just got bored easily.

The afternoon on the estate passed in a blur. Before Molly knew it, Dave announced that it was time to go. The young people began to troop through the doors, apart from one or two who wanted 'one last game', and needed a slightly more assertive approach to get them to leave. With the generator off and everything packed away, Dave closed the doors and brought the engine protesting into life.

Molly leaned back into her seat as the bus pulled away and headed back to the church. She felt exhausted, but in a good way. It was the feeling of a job well done. It had been hard work. She'd struggled to find anything in common with the kids on the bus. She knew their lives were just so different from hers. But now she'd met them, now they were more than faceless people in her imagination, she knew for certain that God cared about them. It was great to know that she'd done something, however small, to show them that.

That evening, all three teams came together to run an open café in the church's community centre. The doors were thrown open, allowing the music from the live band and the tempting aromas of fresh coffee and cakes to waft into the High Street.

For the young people and their leaders, this was the culmination of a long day serving people in their community. It was a chance to chat to anyone who wandered in from the street, and Calvin was relieved to finally get the chance to have a real conversation about God with someone.

But the evening was also a chance to relax a little and to reflect on the day. Some of the volunteers, like Calvin, were buzzing about what they'd seen and done. Others, like Gary, were tired, but with new insights into how powerfully God could work through them. Still others, like Molly, had had a hard day but knew more than ever how important this work was. Tomorrow would bring new challenges and new opportunities to serve people in the name of Jesus. They would all be ready.

Commentary

It's amazing how much Jesus seems to care about our everyday needs. The transcendent creator of the universe loves to comfort people, to meet their needs in incredibly practical ways.[6] The wedding at Cana (John 2:1–11) is a remarkable story for a number of reasons. Quite apart from the miracle of turning one liquid into another, far tastier one, what strikes me about this incident is the way in which Jesus meets the needs of the people at the wedding. It would have been a major embarrassment for the bridegroom if the wine ran out in the middle of the party. Indeed, it was not unknown for the bridegroom to be sued under these circumstances![7]

So Jesus, admittedly with a little encouragement from his mother, acts in a strikingly down-to-earth way to meet the bridegroom's need and save his blushes. And what is it that the revellers at the party need? Quite simply, more wine. It's hardly a matter of life and death; more wine will just mean they enjoy the party more. Yet, Jesus still provides for them. And this wine is the best yet (verse 10). Later in John's Gospel, Jesus explains that he came to give us life in all its fullness – a rich, fulfilling, joyful life (John 10:10). His actions in miraculously providing more wine for a party give us a wonderful illustration of that life.

When these young people took action to serve their community, they found the same thing. Jesus loves to meet the needs of ordinary people in ordinary situations. What could be more practical than digging someone's garden for them? And they found that God truly does work supernaturally through ordinary acts. Just turning up on a woman's doorstep with a random collection of rusty tools can be enough to convince her that God is at work and has not forgotten about her.

And what about the servants? How would they have felt as they filled the jars with water, then took some to the master of the banquet? Would they have understood why Jesus was asking them to do this? Or would they have been daunted, wondering how the master of the banquet would react to the contents of his cup? But whatever the servants' feelings, they chose to obey Jesus, and Jesus did something incredible because of their obedience. Likewise, when we choose to obey Jesus and serve people – even when we don't fully understand why he wants us to do it, even when we're unsure how our actions will be received – Jesus can and does do amazing things through us.

Think about...

- What does your community need?
- How can you and your church serve people in your community?
- What will keep you going if serving people begins to feel like hard work?

Chapter 4

Outsiders

It was so hard to be Tom. His life was rubbish! Tom could not recall the last time somebody asked his opinion on anything; certainly not someone his own age. When had anyone bothered to even be civil to him? However, he could instantly bring to mind the bullying episodes he had endured. Bruises and scrapes lined his body, testimony to the amount of abuse he had faced. Just yesterday Tom had been left hanging from a coat hook for twenty minutes. As the coat held him tightly to the hook, his legs were left swinging in the air. As he was left there hanging, he reminded himself that it wasn't his fault he was short. It was so unfair, but now he was left with another problem to confront: he daren't jump off for fear of his mother's wrath if his coat got ripped. So Tom just stayed there hanging from the hook until his Physical Education teacher came past and put him out of his misery.

On other occasions, his bullies favoured a game of shoving Tom into a locker and locking him in for whatever length of time they felt was funniest. He would be squashed into this horrible metal locker, pressed against its cold sides, left waiting for his tormentors to finally get bored and be kind enough to release him. All of these events meant that, on any given day, Tom was terrified of what might happen to him at school. He spent every moment of each school day looking over his shoulder to see who was trying to get him.

It really was hard being Tom. The worst thing for him was that no teacher seemed to want to protect him. They knew full well that he was being habitually targeted. After all, his Head of Year had come to rescue him from a police station just a few weeks earlier. Tom's form group had been on a school trip to London, and were travelling around on the tube when two of the bigger lads in his class had told Tom they'd arrived at their stop. As they faked stepping off the tube train, Tom mistakenly got off, and, sure enough, the automatic doors closed, the train pulled away, and all Tom could see was his classmates pointing at him whilst squealing with hysterics.

Tom was left all alone at Baker Street station. His mum hadn't let him have his own mobile phone, so Tom didn't know what to do. Standing there on the now empty platform, he felt terribly isolated. Helpless, he felt the coldness of a tear starting to roll down his cheek. He headed for an exit, a way out of this maze. Eventually, with the help of a London Underground employee, he made it to the local police station. From there, his Head of Year was called out to collect him.

The biggest problem for Tom was that everyone else seemed to find his turmoil so funny. To them, their pranks – their spiteful acts of bullying – were hilarious. If there was one thing people seemed to enjoy more than bullying Tom directly, it was laughing at him. So, it wasn't long before this started to have dramatic effects on him. Tom's self-esteem was crushed. He had no friends, and as his classmates loved to remind him, 'Your best mate is your dad!' At primary school, Tom had been a high achiever, but since the bullying had started at secondary school, he had disengaged from education. This once gregarious and outgoing eleven-year-old had soon become a withdrawn, fragile and reclusive teenager. The only hope he had was to get through each school day without too much harassment, further embarrassment or adding to his growing collection of different-coloured bruises.

Things were soon to turn a corner for Tom. There was a small youth group that met at a church near his house. Tom had never been to church but when a new family moved in two doors down from him, one of his new neighbours was Jeff. Jeff attended the youth group and as soon as he had met Tom he asked him if he wanted to come to the group that Friday. Tom was stunned. People of his age didn't ever speak to him like that. He had been forced into becoming a loner. Yet here was someone of his own age who not only seemed OK and clearly comfortable with speaking nicely to him, but was now, incredibly, inviting him to do something social. No one had asked him to do anything like this since Jenny's eleventh birthday a fortnight before the end of primary school, and that was three years ago now. Though he was desperate to go, Tom actually turned down the invite. Years of mental peer-group torture had conditioned Tom to steal away, retreat and hide himself to avoid further painful encounters. He had learned to hide away in his shell.

Jeff was unperturbed by Tom's decline, and for the next three weeks, he kept inviting Tom to the Friday night youth club. After further offers were rejected, Jeff finally got Tom to cave in and agree to go. A thrill of excitement ran through Tom's body at the thought of going out. He needed to meet Jeff at seven, so from five o'clock he locked himself away in his room. He stuck a big 'do not disturb' sign on his door and set about preparing for the night ahead. He was so nervous that there was no way he was going to eat anything, and he certainly didn't want to speak to his parents about it.

It had been so long since he had been out with other young people. The first thing Tom did was to slouch down on his bed and think through what he needed to do in order to get ready. He remembered what he used to wear to important social occasions: trousers, a shirt and some smart shoes. This seemed like a safe bet, so Tom set about getting his clothes together. 'After all, that's how you would dress to go out, isn't it? This is church, right?' He put on his best trousers, pulled out a pristinely ironed shirt and buffed his shoes until he could see his own reflection in them. As Tom looked in the mirror, he thought for the first time in years that he looked good.

He looked at his watch – 5:45! For the next hour and a quarter Tom wished away the minutes by pacing around his room or lying perfectly still – anything to make time go faster. When his watch said 6:30, the nerves started to kick in. Tom's stomach was doing gymnastics as he grew more anxious. By the time seven o'clock eventually came around, he was so nervous that he refused to meet up with Jeff. Instead, he begged his dad for a lift.

As his dad's car pulled into the church car park, Tom was overwhelmed with fear. Who was he going to meet in this forbidding church building? Why would these people like him when, clearly, no one else seemed to? What was he doing here? As he went through the big, heavy doors he immediately felt like a fool. Whereas he was dressed for a primary school tea party, the other kids were in jeans, T-shirts and trainers. 'Just like in everything else, I'm the freak who stands out,' thought Tom as he turned around to leave. He felt there was nothing in his life that was free from this perpetual humiliation. As Tom swivelled around to make a fast exit, Jeff shouted, 'Hi, mate!'

'Mate?' thought Tom. 'No one has ever called me that!' Surprised by this, he turned back towards the group.

Jeff introduced him to the other three: 'Tom, this is Hannah, Lucy and Ethan.'

'Er, h-hi,' stuttered Tom nervously. It took so much for him to get that word out.

Tom was flabbergasted that his appearance didn't seem to matter. For once, even he could see that he looked stupid. Here was a fourteen-year-old lad dressed for a children's tea party – or, come to think of it, a funeral – and yet no one was pointing and laughing at the short kid in the stupid clothes. These people were really not as superficial as the other ones he knew. In fact, they weren't as superficial as Tom himself! He revelled in finding himself in an environment in which he was actually accepted for who he was and what he looked like. As the minutes passed, his confidence, demeanour and personality became increasingly positive. For once, Tom was happy just being Tom, and no longer had to stare over his shoulder all the time.

That night at the youth group flew by. Only a few hours ago, as he lay on his bed, he was pleading for time to pass by. It was an amazing night: a heady collection of up-tempo games and activities, with a talk about God, all run with great enthusiasm by two youth leaders, who were so welcoming to Tom. He was always the outcast, yet here none of those rules seemed to apply. At the end of the evening Tom was delighted to stroll back home with Jeff. Gone was the need to hide away in his dad's car, afraid of stepping outside.

'This is what it's like to be a teenager,' he thought. When he got home, he was bursting with enthusiasm. He bounced into the lounge with an energy and vigour that had previously been obviously lacking. The quiet, withdrawn Tom was replaced by someone so bubbly in character, he permanently seemed as if he had consumed too much coffee! When he eventually went to bed, his parents shared this joy with each other. 'It feels like we've finally got our son back.' They had always been wary of religion, but anything that reinvigorated their son's character to such an extent was most certainly welcome.

From then on, the highlight of Tom's week was the Friday night club. He traded in his trousers, shirt and polished shoes for jeans, T-shirt and trainers. He felt so at home and was accepted. He had been nervous that when his new friends got to know him a bit more, they would all turn against him. In fact, the opposite happened. He was popular! Lucy said he was funny, Hannah thought him cute, Ethan enjoyed his banter and now Tom and Jeff were simply as thick as thieves. Tom was doing all kinds of things he never knew that he could. Ridiculed every time he put on a sports kit, he discovered that in this new environment he was quite a good footballer. Terrified to try anything new at school for fear of being mocked, here he was happy to learn to paint, rap and even break-dance.

Over the next few months, Tom's whole demeanour changed. He had previously done his utmost to remain invisible. Now things were different. There was a spring in his step, a quiet confidence slowly developing. Even his schoolwork was improving. He began to take pride in his appearance, using wax in his hair and no longer wearing the clothes that his mum picked out for him. Now, he wanted to make his own fashion choices. He was changing in every way but what he most loved was his group of friends. They became a tight unit. On Tuesdays they went to the cinema, on Wednesdays they'd go to one of their houses, Friday night was the youth club, on Saturdays they'd hang out in the local shopping centre and then go out in the evening, and on Sundays Tom had started to accompany them all to church.

Tom's parents were blown away by how much he had changed. It particularly hit them at the next parents' evening when one of his teachers declared: 'This new boy in my class didn't even exist three months ago.' Because four young people had treated him without prejudice, Tom's whole life had been turned around. They didn't see him as their metaphorical punchbag or as an object of ridicule, but instead saw him for who he was – a young man travelling through life with them. Tom was profoundly affected. He started going to church and eventually made a confident step of faith and surrendered his life to Jesus.

Commentary

It's really hard to be an outsider, whether because of bullying or any other reason. Those like Tom are outsiders through no fault of their own, whilst others, such as Zacchaeus, bring it upon themselves by their words or actions. Either way, it is incredibly difficult to be ostracized and placed on the fringe of society. In Luke 19:1–10 Jesus encounters Zacchaeus, a figure hated by most in his community. This was no great surprise, since he was a dishonest, cheating tax collector. Additionally, he wasn't just any old tax collector but the chief tax collector who, more than likely, ran the whole tax system for the region. Here was the boss, the worst of the lot!

Failure to pay tax was dealt with very heavily by an aggressive system of enforcement. Threats of violence were rife, and those making these threats were not afraid to follow through on them where necessary. It's little wonder Zacchaeus was so disliked. But in verse 3 of Luke 19, he wants to see Jesus. He is so desperate to get a look at this guy. Matthew Henry believes this is entirely normal:

> It is natural to us to come in sight, if we can, of those whose fame has filled our ears, as being apt to imagine there is something extraordinary in their countenances; at least, we shall be able to say hereafter that we have seen such and such great men.[8]

Zacchaeus would certainly have heard of Jesus' ever-growing reputation. He may have also heard from his contemporaries that, unlike the rest of society, Jesus didn't immediately reject tax collectors. In fact he welcomed them!

Maybe Zacchaeus secretly hankered after a relationship with God, who, unlike the rest of society, didn't actually view him as a lost cause, an irredeemable sinner. Whatever his full motivation, Zacchaeus was faced with the fact that he was short. So we're presented with a crazy image of an immaculately dressed rich man stuck up a tree in the hope of catching just a glimpse of a scruffy-looking, nomadic teacher from Nazareth. Why was he up that tree? In addition to the obvious fact that this tax collector was vertically challenged, the more important reason was that this crowd hated tax collectors and so they would have been unwilling to let him through: 'Why should he get a look in?' The only way for Zacchaeus to see Jesus was from the safe vantage point of a sycamore tree.

How Jesus then proceeds to treat this outsider must have left the crowd in stunned silence. 'Of all the people to go and dine with on a flying ministry tour stop-off, this tax collector is the worst. He is a sinner!' The name Zacchaeus means 'righteous one'.[9] The irony of this parental aspiration is not lost on us, yet forty years later a man from Nazareth visits Jericho and suddenly their prayers are answered: their son becomes righteous. He remedies his lifestyle as a dishonest tax collector by giving back far more than he owes. No longer need he be an outcast. Jesus welcomes him.

Likewise, our Christian communities must welcome the many people that we – or society – have made into outcasts. Whatever reason there is for people being social outcasts, Jesus wants us to reach out to them in love, like he did for Zacchaeus.

Just as the crowd of people were stunned by Jesus' actions towards Zacchaeus, so too the people of today's world should be blown away by our compassion. The way we treat those whom others despise says so much about who we are as Christians, what we believe and who we follow. It's time we stopped marginalizing people and started welcoming them into the church. Let's embrace people of all types with the love of Christ. Let's see everyone as our brothers and sisters and start treating them accordingly. After all, the Bible says in Galatians 3:28 that 'There is neither Jew nor Greek, slave nor free, male nor female, for you are all one in Christ Jesus.'

The story of the small youth group outlined above is a wonderful example of how we should love all people, irrespective of the superficial things that stop others from caring. We should not conform any longer to the patterns of this world (Romans 12:2) but instead we should create a new way of being that loves all. Let's get rid of the concept of outsiders by making everyone welcome. Let's ditch the superficial divides that society tries to create and that make some people feel entirely inadequate. After all, we follow a God who hung around with lepers, prostitutes and tax collectors. It's about time we made everyone feel wanted, loved and welcome. In Jesus' meeting with Zacchaeus and the way that the small youth group welcomed Tom into their social scene, there is a lesson for us all to learn. Who is there in our communities who no one seems to love? And what exactly are we going to do for them?

Think about...

- Take a moment to say sorry to God for the times when you have made others outsiders. Ask for his forgiveness and for his help to avoid repeating this.
- Make a list of those in your community who no one loves. Ask God to show you how he feels about them, and to help you feel the same.
- Begin to pray for these people and seek practical ways of reaching out to them.

Chapter 5

Healing

It was one of those moments which stays with you for the rest of your life. At the time it seemed completely normal, but every time I've thought about it afterwards, I've seen a little bit more how strange and amazing it was.

When I was about thirteen, me and my mates used to go to this place after school. It was kind of a youth club. There was a pool table and a tuck shop, and it was somewhere warm and dry to go when it was raining. The people who ran it used to take assemblies and Citizenship lessons at our school. We knew they were Christians. They knew we weren't really interested in that. But they still let us come in, and they still seemed to care about how we were doing. And since the only alternative was to hang around in the shopping centre, drinking cider and getting into trouble, we used to go to the club most days.

Looking back, we probably annoyed the leaders quite a lot. Some days we were happy to chat, eat sweets and play pool. Other days we just used to mess about and chuck the pool balls at each other. On days like that, the leaders used to ask us to leave earlier than usual. Looking back, they were surprisingly patient with us. Most other people would have shouted at us, but these guys just calmly asked us to leave.

And of course, there were girls at the club too, which was another reason we went. Stacey and Lydia were gorgeous and we used to show off and try to impress them, like you do when you're thirteen. And then there was Carly. Carly was Stacey's mate. I guess she only came because Stacey came. There couldn't have been any other reason. Carly never played any of the games or anything. She just used to sit and talk to Stacey, Lydia and the leaders. We didn't exactly make life easy for her either. You see, the thing about Carly was, she was a misfit. She wasn't good-looking, in fact she was really overweight. She wasn't clever or funny or fashionable or confident either, so she was a bit of an easy target. One of our favourite parts of an afternoon at the club was teasing Carly. She never had a go at us in return, and she used to go bright red when she was embarrassed. I feel bad about it now, but at the time teasing her was a real laugh.

The only problem with going to the club was the God-slot. Like I said, the leaders were Christians, and they insisted on doing a talk about God every day. The deal was, we came to the club and did what we liked for the rest of the time, and in return we'd listen to what they had to say for ten minutes. Back then, I wasn't interested in God, so I didn't really want to listen. But it seemed like a fair deal for what we got in return. And I found out it was possible to sort-of listen, while at the same time punching the guy sat next to me.

Anyway, this one time, we come to the club as usual, play pool, eat sweets and have a go at Carly. Then it's time for the God-slot. So we sit down and prepare to sort-of listen. Debbie gets up and says: 'OK, let's talk about healing.' This actually sounds interesting. So I start properly listening, instead of sort-of listening. Debbie goes on and says that God cares about us and that he can heal us when something's wrong. Well, that stands to reason, right? If he's God, of course he cares about us, and of course he can heal us. That's what God's for.

But the thing that happened next keeps coming back to me, even years later. Suddenly, Carly pipes up and says to Debbie: 'I've got a bad knee. Can you pray for me?'

I could hardly keep a straight face. Carly was setting herself up for some serious mocking here. I was already starting to think about what I'd say to her afterwards. Debbie says of course they'll pray, and asks Carly what's wrong. I can't remember exactly what she said. It was quite complicated stuff about bones being deformed or muscles being the wrong length or something. Whatever it was, it was bad enough for her not to be able to put her foot flat on the floor.

So the leaders gather around Carly and start praying. They all put their hands on her leg, which looks silly, so me and Darren are giggling to ourselves while they're praying. And after a minute or two – and I'll never forget this – Carly says: 'My knee's burning!' Is that good? Then she moves her knee around and puts her foot flat on the floor.

'Yeah,' she says, 'it's better.'

Is this for real? We all gather round to have a look, and it turns out she's telling the truth. It's really happened. This is incredible.

'Go on,' I say, 'put your leg like that again!'

Like I said, it stands to reason that God heals people. It's what he does. But I'd never seen anything like this before. I'd always kind of thought of God as being in the sky somewhere and only being interested in good people, holy people. But here he was, healing one of us in a youth club on a Thursday afternoon. Wow! And there's no denying this was the real deal. I saw Carly's leg before and after she was prayed for. No way she could have made this up.

So in one way, this was amazing, an absolute miracle. But then, that's what God does, right? He's God, he cares about people, he heals them. So it all feels normal at the same time as being amazing. So after a few minutes, I start looking around for something to do. I turn to talk to Debbie:

'So...' I begin. As I look at her I can tell she's expecting me to say something. Maybe something profound, I don't know. I hesitate for a minute and then I ask: 'Can we play pool now?'

It was only when I started looking back at what happened that day that it dawned on me that I really had seen something special. It was then that the amazingness of Carly getting healed started to hit me. God really did care about us. God really was interested in us. God really was there. And I started getting more and more interested in what that meant for me. Eventually, I became a Christian. The more I found out about God, the more I realized I couldn't get away from the fact that he was real and he was interested in me. If that was true, I wanted to know him.

No doubt about it, you can trace me becoming a Christian right back to that ordinary Thursday. Since then, I know I haven't really lived the way a Christian is supposed to live. But every time I remember Carly and the way God healed her, I know that God is still there and still cares about me. However much I mess up, I know he won't give up on me, and deep down, I'll never give up on him. That moment when Carly was healed seemed perfectly normal at the time, but honestly, life has never been the same since.

It was one of those moments where you say something and then you think 'Oh no. These guys are actually going to take this seriously!' When you tell a group of teenagers that God can do something, they tend to take God at his word. So when I uttered the immortal words: 'OK, let's talk about healing,' I suppose I should have known what would happen next.

We'd been running a drop-in youth club for a few months. We reckoned it was a good idea to give the local kids somewhere safe to go and something constructive to do. After all, home was a difficult place for most of them. And also, it was a real opportunity to tell them about Jesus, and we realized they wouldn't get too many opportunities to hear about him otherwise. They'd never set foot in a church. The usual clientele was a group of about twelve or thirteen boys and three girls. The girls would sit in a corner and chat. The boys would play pool and take the mickey out of Carly.

Every day we'd have some kind of 'God slot'. In theory this was quite simple. One of us on the team would say something about God, then everyone would spend a few minutes talking about it. In practice, the 'God slot' was usually ten minutes of chaos, while we tried to keep the kids focused on what we were doing. Before this particular afternoon, it was quite rare for them to show genuine interest in God. So I, for one, didn't expect what happened.

On the fateful Thursday afternoon, we ran back to the youth centre from the school, where we'd been taking a Citizenship lesson. There were three of us: me and Paul and Steph, the year-out volunteers. As we opened the door, glowing slightly from the brisk walk, I checked my watch. We had precisely seven minutes before we needed to open the drop-in. A challenge, but we'd set up in a shorter time than this before. We set up the pool table and the table tennis table, grabbed a few games from the cupboard, and got the tuck out. I had just enough time to mumble a quick prayer before we opened up. On reflection, we probably should have spent a bit longer praying. I think I really knew that at the time, but it just didn't happen. We just didn't have time.

The time came for the 'God slot'. After a couple of minutes' banter and cajoling, we managed to get twelve or thirteen boys and two girls sat down and at least vaguely listening to what we had to say. So far, so good. I can't remember exactly what I said, but something along the lines of: 'Well, God cares about us, he cares about little things, and he can heal us if we ask him' would have escaped my lips. Quite what I thought would happen next, I'm not sure. I probably expected everyone to nod, start losing interest and go back to playing pool and ridiculing Carly. But that wasn't what happened.

While I was in mid-flow, I heard a voice: 'I've got a bad knee. Can you pray for me?' It was Carly. I was gobsmacked. My mind started racing. My first thought was to wonder what possessed Carly to ask that question. Surely she was just inviting more abuse with a request like that. And then I started doing some rapid mental calculations. How bad was Carly's knee problem? How much of a disappointment would it be if God didn't heal her? Was there any way we could start praying for Carly and just keep going until all the boys lost interest? One thing was for sure. After what I'd just said about God, we had to at least pray for her.

So, brimming over with faith and confidence in the Lord, I said brightly: 'Yeah, we can pray for you. What's wrong with your knee?'

And Carly explained. She told us that there was something wrong with the bones in her leg. The way the bones were deformed meant that she couldn't actually put her foot flat on the floor. She showed us what she meant. Sure enough, her foot sat at an awkward angle. Carly explained that she'd never been able to do this. Her leg had been this way since she was born and the doctors had gloomily promised her lots of surgery in the years to come to put her knee right. Even then, the doctors didn't think they'd ever fix it properly. So could we pray for her?

'Ah,' I thought. 'OK. So we're not praying for a headache then? This is going to be fun.'

By this stage, we had a highly attentive audience. All the boys were leaning in, watching to see what we were going to do. I'd never seen them this interested before. Part of me wished they'd just carry on being distracted and apathetic. No such luck. For once, they were hanging on every word I said.

So what could we do? I decided the 'spiritual

bluff' was our best option. We would start praying, the other kids would lose interest and wander off, until it was just us and Carly left. Then we would give her shoulder a meaningful squeeze and reassure her that we'd keep praying for her afterwards.

So we started praying for her. We prayed for a couple of minutes. I opened one eye slightly. Everyone was still watching. One or two of the boys had their eyes closed too. This was not quite going according to plan. I began to wonder if any of the young people would listen to a word I said about God after this. Then...

'My knee's burning!' Carly exclaimed, sounding surprised rather than in pain.

'Really?!' I asked – full of faith, as ever.

'Wow!' I thought, 'Something's actually happening!' After another couple of minutes, we finished praying. Carly told us how her leg was meant to be aligned. She flexed her knee once or twice.

'Yeah,' she said nonchalantly, 'it's better.'

What?

I wanted to say: 'What do you mean, "It's better"?! This is something you needed major surgery for!' I watched open-mouthed as Carly stretched her legs out in front of her, then bent her knees and put both feet flat on the floor.

'Yeah,' Carly went on, 'I can do that now. Cool! Thanks!'

'And... and you definitely couldn't do that before?'

Paul asked tentatively.

'Oh no. My muscles were all the wrong length, you see. Because of the way the bones were deformed. No, I couldn't do this before.'

You could have heard a pin drop. I didn't know what to say. I was trying to act as though I had expected this all along. I don't think I really fooled anyone. I looked at Paul and Steph. Their bottom jaws were practically on the floor.

'Let's see,' Darren said, and stepped forward.

The boys all moved forward and crowded around Carly. For once, they weren't mocking her.

'Wow! That's amazing!'

'No way!'

'Go on, put your leg like that again!'

Again, my mind was racing. This was incredible! Surely the kids would realize now that everything we'd been telling them about God was true. Surely they'd all become Christians. They'd have to now, wouldn't they? I had visions of the lot of them on their knees, weeping in repentance and giving their lives to the Lord. But once again, that wasn't quite how it played out.

For a few minutes, the excitement in the room was intense. Everyone was standing around Carly, chatting, poking and prodding her leg, and occasionally saying how amazing this all was. Then it all went quiet again. This was it. This was the moment. This was when they would all give their lives to Jesus. Right?

Kieron turned to me. 'So...' he began.

Go on, Kieron. Just ask. Ask what you have to do to be saved.

'Can we play pool now?'

'What?' I asked blankly. Did he really say what I thought he said?

'Can we play pool now?' he repeated, slightly nervously.

Play pool?! After what just happened?! You've just seen the most amazing healing you're ever likely to see in your life, and you want to go and play pool?!

'Yeah, OK.' I smiled weakly.

The last twenty minutes before we closed passed in a blur. Carly and Stacey went home. Carly was buzzing and wanted to show her parents her newly functional leg. The boys went back to the pool table. Paul, Steph and I stayed rooted to the spot for probably a full five minutes, trying to make sense of it all. A few minutes of simple prayer. No great faith. No great feeling of God's presence with us. No fasting, repentance of every known sin or anything else that's supposed to make healing more likely. But then an absolutely awesome miracle. Possibly the most awesome miracle the three of us had ever seen. And the kids saw God do something like that – and then they went back to playing pool.

Things changed at the drop-in after that. All the young people who came were more interested in talking about God. And when someone in one of their families was ill, they'd always ask us to pray for them now. There was something different about them when we looked at them, too. Something that I couldn't quite put my finger on. Perhaps a little more sparkle in their eyes or something. This was great, but the three of us were frustrated that the changes in the kids weren't more dramatic. Weren't they supposed to become Christians now?!

Carly's been fine since. She went for a check-up at the hospital soon afterwards, and came to tell us what happened. Sure enough, the bones and the muscles were exactly as they should have been. The doctor confirmed that she wouldn't need surgery. So just in case we were wondering whether we'd imagined the whole thing... Carly thought it was brilliant that she'd been healed. So did her parents. It didn't make her want to become a Christian, at that stage anyway – which, of course, was frustrating. But we just had to trust that God had a plan for her, and that this had just been a small part of it. At any rate, it was obvious that God had his hand on her life.

I often think back to that Thursday afternoon. I still wonder why God chose that point to do something amazing. We hadn't prayed particularly hard beforehand. There was no 'OK, everyone, let's really focus on God now.' There was no rise in my faith; no feeling that something extraordinary was coming. But despite our complete lack of faith, despite our complete lack of preparation, God chose to heal Carly anyway.

And I wonder how the kids could see a physical healing like that and not be convinced to give their lives to God on the spot. I suppose they took what we said at face value. We told them that God heals. We prayed for Carly. She got better. So in their minds, the healing proved that what we'd said was true. But it didn't make them immediately think of becoming Christians. For a bunch of thirteen- and fourteen-year-olds who'd never been to church, that would have been a huge leap to make. And why should they have been surprised by seeing a healing? They'd had no experience of the number of times a person prays for healing and nothing seems to happen.

The Bible says that signs and wonders will accompany our preaching. It's the truth that sets people free. Perhaps the healing was just a sign for the young people, something to point them towards God. Perhaps as they got to know God and his truth better, that was what set them free and made them want to follow him. And perhaps the lesson in Carly's healing was more for us than for the young people. Perhaps it was simply a moment of God breaking into our routine, breaking into our cynicism and our assumptions about what he could and would do. Perhaps God just wanted to say to us: 'Yeah. I can.'

Commentary

God seems to have a habit of blowing away people's preconceived ideas of how and when he works. Just when we get comfortable, and we think we know what to expect of God, he seems to do something that comes as a complete surprise. The youth leaders in this story certainly found that. Despite their own weaknesses, despite their failure to follow the formulas they thought would make it more likely for God to work, God did something incredible. And it was the leaders, the people who'd been trying to live for God for years, who seemed to find the whole thing hard to deal with!

The fact is, God does love his children, and he does love to heal us. The youth leaders' theology was absolutely right! But it's easy to forget simple truths like these if you've been disappointed before, or to attach all sorts of conditions to them, which almost create the idea that you have to make yourself good enough to deserve to be healed. To the youth leaders, who'd been Christians for years, seeing a healing was staggering. To Carly, with her simple faith in God, it was no surprise at all.

In John chapter 9, we find a very similar situation. An ordinary man with a very real physical problem is healed by Jesus. There's nothing about this man in the narrative to say he was particularly righteous. In fact, the disciples speculate about exactly how sinful the man is! And yet, Jesus chooses to heal him. He shows that he values a man who other people have disregarded and written off as sinful. And Jesus heals the man 'so that the work of God might be displayed in his life.' Maybe Jesus heals people just because he loves them, and just so that God's work can be seen in their lives. Seeing one of his children suffer moves Jesus to act and heal.[10] And maybe Jesus heals people like Carly because they're not afraid to ask.

Like the youth leaders in the story, the Pharisees were stunned to see a miracle like this. They weren't just surprised, they couldn't actually believe that it was from God because it happened in such a surprising way, and completely obliterated their ideas of who could be healed and how it would happen. As one writer puts it, Jesus 'shakes our old ideas of morality, and helps us to understand God's righteousness.'[11]

So at what point does the man Jesus heals become a Christian? Verse 25 suggests that he doesn't really understand who Jesus is or how he has healed him. We're merely left with his simple but profound testimony: 'One thing I do know. I was blind, but now I see!' But verses 27 and 28 imply that he already considers himself a disciple of Jesus. It seems that this is something of a faith journey for the man. It's only later on, in verse 38, following another conversation with Jesus, that the man truly recognizes who Jesus is and worships him. The healing was a sign which pointed the man to the truth of who Jesus is.

And what about Carly? She certainly didn't make any great profession of faith just after she was healed. It's unlikely she really had much understanding of who Jesus was at that stage. Her testimony, like the blind man's, would probably have been very simple: 'All I know is, my leg was deformed. Now it isn't!' Carly's healing was a sign that pointed her and the other kids at the drop-in to the truth of who Jesus is.

Think about...

- Do you or someone you know need a touch of God's healing power?
- This might sound like a silly question, but have you prayed for healing?
- Are you willing to accept that God might not work in the ways you expect?

Chapter 6

Values

No one would have guessed that the way one young woman chose to spend a year of her life would have a profound effect on her entire youth group. Lisa had grown up in one of the most affluent parts of England. She was from a strong Christian background and was keen to discover other parts of the world for herself. She really wanted to see something different and experience how others lived. So, on turning eighteen, she went on a gap year to Uganda. She had an incredible time and was full of mixed emotions about returning home. She was looking forward to going home, but she was uncomfortably aware that what she had seen and experienced had changed her forever.

Once back in the familiar surroundings of England, Lisa could not accept a 'matter of fact' return to British society and spoke with great vigour and passion about all she had seen. Anyone who would listen would be told about her adventures and the immense needs of the Ugandan people. Her infectious enthusiasm provided a powerful catalyst for getting others excited, passionate and involved. She quickly had a strong impact on her peers.

Soon enough, the local youth leaders were organizing a trip to Uganda for the whole youth group to get an opportunity to see some of what Lisa had been so passionate about. To the surprise of the organizers, some thirty young people desperately wanted to go. While one might expect a heavy dose of compassion fatigue from materialistic, self-centred teenagers, instead this gang of young people needed little persuading and were in no way inhibited by the £1,000 they would each be required to raise. With gusto, they set about coming up with creative ideas for raising money and eagerly began looking forward to their trip.

An in-depth eleven-month training programme kicked in, preparing the young people for what lay ahead. This comprehensive course was delivered by youth leaders, by Ugandans living in England, and by Christians experienced in cross-cultural work. The training was fascinating and the young people lapped it up.

It was only as the trip drew closer that the nerves began to kick in. Fearful parents were questioning the safety and wisdom of it all. Teenagers were starting to watch images of suffering on the news and realized that soon enough they would be there amongst those people, right in the thick of the action. Creature comforts of postmodern Western society would be replaced with a voyage into the unknown. Would there even be showers? What would they eat? Where would they sleep? What dangerous animals might attack them? What about disease? One teenager even wondered how she would be able to plug in and use her GHD hair straighteners!

There was one young girl in particular who was clearly quite afraid. She knew that she had to go and yet spent hours sobbing on her youth leaders' sofa. The tears didn't dry up even as the coach travelled towards the airport. She only properly stopped crying as the air hostess came round with drinks and peanuts. There was now no possibility of turning back, so her tears seemed futile and soon dried up. For this youth group bunched up together in economy class, the atmosphere on the flight was a potent blend of anxiety, dread, expectation and excitement. The flight went by in a flash and as the wheels of the plane touched the tarmac in Kampala, the adventure was only just beginning.

It was Saturday, everyone was tired, and after they had seen a local dance show, bed provided a welcome relief. The next day this affluent youth group from a small, traditional Anglican church would experience church, African style. The young people were blown away as they walked into a large throng of worshippers. The music was loud, but melodic. The worship was chaotic, but strangely peaceful. As they looked around they were stunned at the joy of the people. These folk really loved God, and this appeared to be truly heartfelt worship. There was an incredible, tangible sense of God's presence – something all too rare in services back home. The service here was long, but it seemed to pass in an instant. Without exception, they were challenged by the kind of church they had seen. They too wanted to worship God with such joy, no matter what was going on 'behind the scenes' in their lives.

The settling-in period was over and the next day it was time for the work to start. Over the next few weeks they were to be split into teams and would rotate around three different centres, spending a week in each. The work was plentiful and varied. For a start, there were the action-packed holiday clubs for children. The age range was vast – three to fifteen. It struck the young people how fortunate they were in Britain, where the largest age group would be eleven to fourteen or fourteen to eighteen. Yet back in England they would moan that these age groups were too wide. They would certainly think twice before raising this complaint again! Daily attendance at the holiday clubs ranged from 40 to 100 children. The people's first language wasn't English, so it was very challenging. However, some things – football, craft, laughter – transcended any language barriers.

There were also lessons to be taught in schools. These teenagers had suddenly gone from being taught themselves to teaching others. English, Maths,

Religious Education... the mixture was interesting but it was a privilege to pass on some of what their expensive Western education had taught them. At first, everything seemed easier than they had thought it would be. Life wasn't all that hard for the young people, who went to nice holiday clubs and received a good education. However, the truth beneath this shiny veneer of an easy life would soon be revealed. As time passed and relationships began to be established, the Ugandan children started to tentatively share their stories. A great sense of suffering soon became clear in each of their lives.

One third of the school were Aids orphans, and though they had some food every day, it was nothing like the Western 'eat as much as you can' diet. Each story that was heard began to unveil a web of suffering that these poor Ugandan people had faced. It seemed so unjust! Someone's chances in life seemed completely dependent on where that person was born. While the English teenagers had private education, bottled sparkling mineral water and fashion icons, their Ugandan counterparts were privileged to have any education, drank whatever water was available (if any) and wore any clothes they could get hold of. The English teenagers began to be hit by the sheer enormity of the need. However, they were hugely encouraged by the fact that they could make a difference. They would not glibly accept that because the task of helping these people was so huge, it simply was not even worth trying. After all, they'd all heard the famous saying that 'A journey of a thousand miles begins with a single step.' These teenagers knew that the little they could do would at least begin to make a difference.

As well as the teaching, the boys, in particular, were delighted to be involved in doing some practical work. They built a bridge, did some carpentry work, cleared drains, built a mud hut, cleaned out a waterhole – the list seemed endless! It was so rewarding to be able to help in such a practical way. Particularly moving for the group was the chance of building a home for a woman. The overwhelmed look on her face as she gazed at her new home was something the teenagers would never forget. In such a short space of time, without too much effort and at such a small financial cost, they had managed to build a house for someone who had never had one before. This made them appreciate their lavish family homes back in England.

They had one life-changing experience after another. Being able to practically help those in need was a rollercoaster ride of emotions. On the one hand was great joy at improving people's lives; yet on the other, there were slight tinges of guilt about all they had back home, in comparison to these people. They were deeply challenged by seeing local children drinking water that was so dirty, it looked more like Coca-Cola. Yet their practical efforts would help purify that water, allowing local people to drink clean water instead. The youth group would never drink water – or Coca-Cola – as glibly again.

The final element of their hands-on work was helping to lead large Sunday schools. This was really enjoyable. Ever since that early visit to the church, the group had struggled with what seemed a bizarre dichotomy of incredible worship and thankfulness to God and the everyday reality of poverty, hardship and disease. Those strange biblical riddles such as 'Blessed are you who are poor, for yours is the kingdom of God' (Luke 6:20) and 'It is easier for a camel to go through the eye of a needle than for a rich man to enter the kingdom of God' (Mark 10:25) suddenly started to make sense. It did seem so much easier for these people, who had so little, to turn and worship God. They had a simple choice: to depend on God or to despair, as God was really all that they had. The English young people had everything that this world had to offer, and yet this seemed to make it harder to worship Jesus and be full of joy, not easier. The joy of people living through terrible suffering was impossible to ignore. The English group were left philosophizing that 'money can't buy you happiness.' 'If only our lives were less cluttered, then we might get closer to Jesus,' they observed.

During their stay in Uganda, time seemed to pass by at three or four times the speed of normal life. As the trip drew to an end, the group had all been hugely impacted. One member reflected, 'I thought I was coming here to help poor people on the other side of the world. However, I have learnt far more from them then I could ever have hoped.' Another put it even more succinctly: 'I will never be the same again.' When we live in a world that is so openly scathing of young people and their attitudes, it is amazing to find that many are simply not like our media stereotype. Here was a group who had been profoundly affected and now wanted to help change the world. These are certainly not the media-caricatured 'hoodies'. And it was not just the young people who were transformed. A vastly experienced youth worker who went with them said, 'In twenty-five years of youth work, this is the most rewarding and challenging thing I have ever been involved in.'

As they landed back in England, it was hard to know what long-term effects, if any, this trip would have upon their lives. Would the effects last a week, a couple of months, or possibly even a year? How long would it really be until normal service resumed and these young people slipped back into their previous lifestyles? Surely the lessons learnt would be easily lost and Africa would become little more than a fading memory. But no, this would not be the case for this dynamic group of young people. Just as Lisa had returned from Uganda unable to keep what she had seen to herself, now the whole group knew that they had to spread the message of what each of them had witnessed with their own eyes. As one girl put it, 'We simply cannot allow ourselves to have witnessed what we have seen and go home and do nothing.'

Both collectively and individually, the group were thinking through the many things they could do. Some solutions were obvious. They had to help more children get fresh water. So money was raised for this, and now 3,000 people in the village have clean water every day. What a change for each of those individuals. Though this was an amazing development, it simply wasn't enough. 'Surely we can do more for these people,' the group would tell each other, as they continued to make plans.

With help from some of their youth leaders, the young people went so far as establishing a charitable trust to help an impoverished school in Uganda. Three of the young people from the trip are youth advisers to this trust and attend all the trustees' meetings. So far the trust has managed to raise in excess of £30,000, and it has been established and operational for less than a year! To think that our society can be so negative about what is possible, yet here is a bunch of young people who simply aren't prepared to accept that those they met in Uganda have to go without so much. Instead of just feeling sorry for those struggling people, this group have got off their backsides and made a real difference. So much for so-called 'compassion fatigue'!

As well as their corporate action, some of

the group have felt compelled to make individual responses. One girl built up a relationship with a family in Uganda and was so struck by their need that, to help support them, she has begun selling jewellery in Britain produced by the family in Uganda. So far she has been able to send the family well over £300. Another young person made an incredible response. For her eighteenth birthday she asked to be given money instead of presents. Her friends and family obliged and were stunned to discover that she gave every penny of this away to help children in Uganda! This would have been unthinkable prior to her trip and sounds like lunacy to most of her peers. Other members of the group have made sure that their school has taken on the trust as its official charity. This has meant that fund-raisers such as 'Own Clothes Days' have resulted in more much-needed money being sent to Uganda.

The responses made by the youth group have not simply been limited to finance. Members of the group have taken assemblies in their schools to raise awareness and have even invited someone from Uganda to be involved in this. Each of the young people have grown in their faith and developed. They all have a deeper and stronger Christian conviction than before the trip. Equally, they have begun to understand God's value system and not just that of their own Western society. Career choices have changed, families have been impacted, and the church they have returned to will never be allowed to ignore Uganda again. The teenagers themselves have learnt things from the Ugandan people that they want to put into effect here, not least the need for stronger community in England.

The group were able to make a real difference in Uganda. There is now a strong link formed and a second team are going out soon. However, even if nothing was achieved in Uganda, it would have been worth it for their own lives to be challenged and changed. This group of teenagers will simply never be the same again.

Commentary

In John chapter 13, Jesus and his disciples have sat down for dinner. But there's a problem! They've been on a long journey beforehand and have not yet had their feet washed. This would be deemed highly impolite and it was entirely inappropriate to eat a meal at your host's house without previously having your feet washed. In their *Bible Knowledge Commentary*, Walvoord and Zuck point out that 'Foot-washing was needed. The streets were dusty and people wore sandals without socks. It was a mark of honour for a host to provide a servant to wash a guest's feet; it was a breach of hospitality not to provide for it.'[12] So there was a problem: it was time for food, stomachs were rumbling, and yet feet were dirty.

Foot-washing was deemed to be a job for the lowest of the low, as it was such a horrid, humbling and demeaning task. Milne tells us that foot-washing is 'Included in a list of works which a Jewish slave should not be required to perform.'[13] Therefore the only sort of person considered low enough to wash feet was a Gentile slave. In John 13 there was clearly no Gentile slave available, otherwise their feet would have been washed.

As Jesus and his disciples sat around, knowing their food was going cold, they were faced with a real dilemma. They couldn't eat without their feet being washed but there was no one to wash their feet. The disciples wouldn't have dreamt for one moment about washing one another's feet. This would be a peer-to-peer act. It was unthinkable in their society that peer-to-peer feet-washing would ever take place. As they all sat around not knowing what to do, Jesus, the King of the world – who in the words of the modern hymn, 'flung stars into space'[14] – behaved as a Servant King. He got up from his seat and in one awe-inspiring moment, grabbed a towel and a bucket and washed each of his disciples' feet.

Jesus was above them in rank and yet was prepared to act as the lowest servant and wash their feet. In one incredible moment, he reversed the economy of the world that tells us to chase after money, status and success. In their place Jesus instead instils an altogether different value system of mercy, service and love. What a contrast! As Christians it is so important that we don't get caught up chasing the values of this world, but instead go running after Jesus and that which he shows us really matters. Jesus' actions were meant as an example. If he can lower himself to wash his disciples' feet, then we should have no hesitation in doing the same for others.[15]

When those young people went to Uganda, their whole value system was transformed. As with the disciples when Jesus washed their feet, so with this youth group, as the whole focus of their lives was transformed in Uganda. They began to see things through the eyes of Jesus, as opposed to the Western culture they'd grown up in. We as a church have got to turn our backs on the values inherited from Western society and embrace the value system of this Servant King. Jesus is not an aloof King, obsessed with position and power, but a Servant King, always prepared to do the unlikely, and always motivated by love; a King with compassion for everyone in every situation. Let's not be a selfish, 'compassion fatigued', Western group of believers, but instead an open, loving, humble, caring, hope-filled and hope-expressing church community, partnering with God in his mission to the world.

T h i n k   a b o u t ...

- What set of values do you really live by? Is your bank balance more important than the plight of your brother or sister on the other side of the world?
- When you see people struggling within other countries on the news, how do you react? Are you compassion fatigued? What can you do to jolt yourself out of this? When did you last ask God to help you view people differently?
- Is there something you or your church should be doing practically to help those around the world who are in desperate need?

Chapter 7

Next Step

The leaders stood silently and cast their eyes over the aftermath of the youth club. The floor of the church hall was covered in crisp crumbs, shredded paper and candle-wax. Out in the lobby, there was a large coffee stain on the carpet, which, despite their best efforts, they hadn't been able to completely remove. The broken vase and the remains of the flower arrangement had been swiftly moved to the dustbin. And the aroma in the building was a faint but distinct mixture of marijuana smoke and sweat masked by a pungent deodorant.

Toby glanced at Karen. She looked exhausted. It struck him how young she was; only a few months older than some of the club's members. How could she be expected to deal with something like this? And how could she be expected to lead a team through it?

'Karen, we can't go on like this,' Toby said gently. 'If we carry on, someone's going to end up getting killed.' He paused. This sounded more melodramatic than he'd wanted. 'And you know what the church wardens would say about blood on the carpet...'

Karen smiled wryly.

'Toby's right, though,' Sarah agreed. 'The club is getting more chaotic every week. It's only a matter of time before something really bad happens and we have to call the police. I only just talked Rob out of throwing a chair through the window tonight. He's getting harder and harder to handle. And he's not the only one.' Sarah didn't add that she'd nearly been knocked across the room by Rob's flailing fists in the build-up to the stand-off over the chair.

Karen sighed. She'd put so much time, energy and prayer into making the club work. She knew the rest of the team had too. And it had been brilliant. Some of the young people who came had been utterly transformed in the time she'd known them. How could she even think about closing the club down? But lately it had all been such a slog. No one seemed interested in God any more. The young people were far more excited about making a mess, drinking cider outside the church, and generally causing a nuisance. It was all so frustrating. She looked at the faces of the other leaders. They were tired, exasperated and disillusioned. What were they supposed to do? She felt her eyes fill with tears. She felt so useless.

'Let's clean this place up,' Karen said glumly.

The youth club was now unrecognizable from how it had been just a few months previously. Some of the changes were wonderful. Others definitely were not.

For as long as the leaders could remember, the youth club had been... well... nice. The teenagers who came were mostly Christians, or at least polite, friendly and apparently well balanced. They'd come, drink coffee and chat, perhaps play some table tennis, listen to someone talk about God for ten minutes, then go home.

That all changed on one fateful Friday night, when a completely different crowd strode into the church hall. They were dressed almost totally in black, down to the hair dye, eyeliner and lipstick that even the boys in the gang felt was necessary. There were only seven of them, but something about them gave the impression that they numbered at least twelve.

The regulars in the group stopped what they were doing and watched the newcomers as they came in. There was an awkward silence. One of the black-clad boys fumbled in his pocket for a cigarette.

'Anyone got a light?' he asked nonchalantly.

The leaders exchanged bemused looks. Nobody seemed to know why these visitors were there. Toby stepped forward.

'You'll have to go outside if you want to smoke, mate. Er... do you want a cup of tea?'

The rest of the evening continued in a similarly awkward way. The regulars and the newcomers kept to their own friendship groups, hardly speaking to each other, and the leaders did the best they could to make the newcomers feel welcome in an environment that was clearly completely alien to them. It all felt very strange.

None of the leaders really expected to see the boys and girls in black again, but the following Friday, they returned. And the Friday after that. Suddenly, unexpectedly, the club had nearly doubled in size.

Nobody seemed to know why the new members of the club had come. Karen vaguely remembered chatting to some of them after she'd given an assembly at the local school. And now she thought about it, she'd spoken to them a few times, while she was doing detached youth work, talking to young people who were hanging around in the streets. Toby and Stuart had seen the group sitting outside the church once or twice, and had stopped to say hello. Somewhere along the line, somebody had obviously told them: 'We've got a thing on at the church on Friday night. You can come along if you like.' But none of the leaders could remember having said that.

Still, one way or another, these very different young people had found the church and started making themselves at home. The first couple of months were, to put it mildly, a learning experience for all concerned. The invisible barrier between the two factions in the club began to break down. To the leaders' surprise, the 'nice' young people made a real effort to befriend the slightly intimidating ones, even though before this point they would probably have seen the same people at school and tried to stay out of their way. And the unexpected newbies responded well. Underneath their unnerving appearance, they revealed themselves to be friendly towards the existing group members, mostly respectful towards the leaders, and willing to join in with the club activities. But the best part of this for the leaders was that these young people who'd never previously set foot in a church were genuinely interested in God. They listened carefully to the talks, they were brimming over with questions about life, God and the world, and they even joined in with the club's prayer times. The leaders were delighted!

Karen was especially excited. As she got to know the new arrivals, she began to see herself in them. Watching them and talking to them brought up still-fresh memories of where she'd come from and how her life had been just a few short months before. But since then, miraculously, God had broken into her life and completely turned her around. And this was exactly why she was now doing youth work. She knew that God could change people, however far they seemed from him. When she saw the youth club's surprising new clientele, she was reminded of her own experience of God's amazing power to transform lost people. Just thinking about what could happen next made Karen grin.

Unfortunately, there were difficulties which accompanied the new arrivals too. Their penchant for heavy drinking and recreational drugs might not have been a big issue – might even have been something the leaders could ignore – if the teenagers didn't insist on indulging directly before coming to the youth club. On any given Friday night, it was difficult to predict what kind of state some of them would be in, and therefore how easy they would be to handle, because it was conditional on what they'd been taking immediately beforehand! On occasions, the group would be discovered sitting outside the church before the club opened, drinking cider and smoking pot. This became an even bigger problem when one or two of the 'churched' kids were tempted to join them.

In the case of one particular young man, it was almost a relief when he did turn up under the influence. Rob turned out to be a great guy with an infectious sense of humour and a sharp, inquiring mind. He also turned out to have huge anger-management issues. His family life and problems at school had combined to make him extremely angry, frustrated and hurt. Rob's anger could flare up at the least apparent provocation, and was very hard to deal with when it came to the fore. Often, the only solution was to leave Rob alone in a room until he'd calmed down, or to send him to stomp around the park for a few minutes. Marijuana was by no means the solution to his deep-rooted problems, but at least it made him more placid in the short term.

And then there was Sally. She was the natural leader of her cohorts, and probably more intimidating than anyone else in the group. Sally was highly intelligent, highly unpredictable and highly manipulative. Starved of attention at home, she'd become expert at winning attention in other places, including the youth club, regardless of whatever else was going on. This generated some bad feeling within the club, especially when some of the girls got to know Sally better, and found that she manipulated them and let them down too.

It became clear to Karen and her team just how hurt and broken the new members of the club were. They came from well-off, middle-class families. They wanted for nothing as far as material possessions were concerned. And yet, life had still left them deeply hurt, damaged and insecure. The leaders began to realize that this was the root of all the anger, drinking and manipulative behaviour. And as they realized this, they began to care about Rob, Sally and the others very deeply. They reminded Karen vividly of her recent past and old friends. Not so long ago, she'd been in a hauntingly similar position. Her life had been centred around drink, drugs and unhealthy relationships, as she tried to escape the pain and emptiness she felt. But meeting God had changed everything. And these hard, marginalized young people, who reminded her so much of herself, were just beginning to get closer to him. The whole team were moved to pray for them and spend time with them, but Karen felt this intensely. She felt herself being pulled in different directions as she tried to lead the teenagers and deal with their challenging behaviour, while at the same time desperately wanting to reach out to them as a friend.

The leaders' prayers were soon answered dramatically. The new members of the group began to change. As they got closer to God, everything about them changed. Rob's bursts of anger became less fierce and less frequent. Sally became more open and less manipulative. The drinking and drug-taking got less and less frequent. The discussions about God became more intense and meaningful. On occasions, one or two of the club's committed new members were literally left in tears of repentance at the end of a meeting. And finally, one by one, they began to surrender their lives to God and become Christians. There was no doubt about it: God was transforming broken, hurt and angry young people. It was absolutely wonderful. Karen was overjoyed.

For a couple of months, the wonderfulness continued. The boundaries between the two 'tribes' within the club blurred, as everyone seemed united in a desire to get closer to God and bring their lifestyle in line with his will. The atmosphere within the group had changed dramatically. One or two of the new converts were even thinking about doing a year out with a Christian charity.

Then, one Friday, Sally, Rob and the others

weren't there. Karen was surprised, but not too concerned, and the club went ahead as usual. The following Friday, they were back. And without warning, without any apparent reason, they were back to their old habits. Suddenly, Rob was angry again, Sally was as manipulative as ever, and the drinking and pot-smoking were back in force. It was almost as though the previous two or three months had never happened. Perhaps this was just a blip? Sadly, no. In the weeks afterwards, the club returned to a familiar pattern, except that the new converts had discovered some other forms of unpleasant behaviour too. Along with the old drinking, anger and disregard for church property, they had become very demanding. They seemed to want the leaders to be available to pray for them as soon as they wanted prayer, and then to leave them alone as soon as they wanted to be left alone. To make matters worse, the old guard in the group began to resent the amount of attention that the newcomers seemed to need. They were used to having the leaders invest time and energy in them, and this just wasn't happening any more. Or at least, not as much.

Karen was baffled and hurt. What had caused the sudden change in the group's behaviour? Was it her? Something she'd said or done? In her heart of hearts she knew she shouldn't take this setback personally, but it was hard not to, when she'd invested so much of herself in the group. In the weeks and months to come, the leaders spoke to almost every member of the group about why things had changed so suddenly. Bizarrely, even the young people themselves couldn't think of a reason.

The whole situation left Karen and her team with a dilemma. Helping a group of young people with such huge problems to live for God was always going to be a difficult and messy exercise. But was it right that this should be at the expense of discipling other young people? The grumbles from the church wardens about the state of the building after the youth club had been in were beginning to get louder. And the vicar was almost press-ganging more church members into helping with the club, just to keep the damage to a minimum. So should they just ban the kids who were causing trouble? No, this would just be piling more rejection onto youngsters who'd experienced more than enough rejection already. And it would make a mockery of the open, inclusive, bring-your-friends message of the club. 'Bring your friends, but only if they're nice.'

So the troublemakers stayed, and the challenging behaviour continued. The extra helpers drafted in by the vicar found themselves policing the club and preventing trouble, rather than developing meaningful relationships with the club members. And if anything, the young people's behaviour got worse and worse. They refused to engage with any activity they weren't immediately interested in. They showed no respect for the church building or the facilities; breakages became common. And there was no way of predicting how they would react to a simple greeting or request. They could be all smiles one minute, sullen and contemptuous the next.

Karen had never felt pressure like this before. She had to deal with how unpredictable the group was, and she also had to handle criticism of how she was running the club from older members of the church. She found that the only answer was to rely on God to make her wise and strong enough to handle it all.

Finally, Stuart suggested closing the club down. To begin with, none of the other leaders wanted to listen to him. They reasoned that if they just persevered, God would do something amazing. After all, he'd utterly transformed these hurting young people before. Why couldn't he do it again? Stuart calmly pointed out that Friday nights had become more about crowd control than discipleship, or even having fun. He suggested that if they kept the club running, they'd risk damaging the young people's relationships with each other, the leaders and God more than if they closed the club down. The other leaders didn't want to hear this; Karen in particular, but Stuart's words played on her mind over the days that followed. Maybe he was right.

But the following Friday night was amazing. Sally and her tribe went along with whatever the leaders asked, interacted brilliantly with the rest of the group, and seemed genuinely enthusiastic about the prayer activities Louise had organized. The evening finished with Neil apologizing to Toby for the way he'd been behaving and asking him to pray for him. Karen was over the moon. Surely the club had turned a corner. They'd persevered through a hard time, and now the teenagers were making real progress with God again.

Karen was brought back down to earth with a bump the following week. The teenagers were as unruly as ever. What followed was nothing short of a rollercoaster ride for the young people and the leaders alike. Again and again the club would become so unruly and relationships so strained that the leaders would be convinced that closing the club down was the only wise option. But repeatedly, as soon as they came to this decision, something brilliant would happen – group members who had been at each other's throats would make up and be the best of friends, a hardened drinker in the group would feel convicted and swear off the cider, or someone would end up weeping with repentance – and the leaders would be convinced that some new activities and a renewed commitment to pray for the group were all that was needed.

Until this particular Friday.

Karen looked up from sweeping up the debris on the church hall floor. As she saw the mess around her, and the tiredness etched on the faces of the rest of the team, she realized that the time had come. They'd tried everything. To keep going now would risk relationships with the young people deteriorating to the point of no return. And Toby was right; there was a very real risk that, sooner rather than later, someone would do something truly awful, and the police would have to be involved. To say nothing of the unsettling effect this was all having on the kids who'd been in the group all along, and the stress and sleepless nights it was costing the leaders. And wouldn't it be better to stop now, while the memories of the good that God had done were still fresh in their minds?

'OK,' Karen said quietly, when the team had finished clearing up. 'Thank you all for your help tonight. Can we meet quickly after church on Sunday morning? We can't go on like this. We need to decide what we're going to do.'

Karen sobbed on the way home. The sudden, lurching ups and downs with the club had left her worn out; physically, emotionally and spiritually. She was going to pray hard about this, but deep down she knew it was time for the club to end.

On Sunday morning, the team came together again.

'Thanks for coming, everyone,' Karen smiled, stirring her tea nervously. 'I want you all to know how much I appreciate your help with the youth club. Whatever happens now, what we've done has made a real difference for the young people, and God really has transformed them.'

She looked up and caught Sarah's eye. Sarah smiled encouragingly. Karen went on.

'There's no easy way of saying this. I think it's time to close the club,' she said baldly. 'As it is, we're not helping anyone. Not the new members, not the old members, not the rest of the church, and not ourselves.'

'So what do you suggest?' Stuart asked. 'I agree with you, by the way, but how do we end this without making everyone feel let down?'

Between them, they made a plan. They'd explain to the young people that the group had to close. It would be unpleasant. They probably would be very disappointed and feel let down, and that was more or less unavoidable. But they'd announce a final event – a night to celebrate what the group had been and what God had done for them. They'd finish with a bang. And they'd mention the Sunday morning youth group – there was no reason why anyone who was interested couldn't come to that. It was a hard decision, extremely hard. But all five of them felt a strange sensation of lightness as they went their separate ways.

On Friday, the leaders told everyone at the youth club what was going to happen. There were tears, from leaders and young people alike. There was confusion and disappointment. This was a wrench for everyone, and there was no getting away from that. But the club had simply run its course. It was time to move on.

The night of the final event came. Nearly everyone from the club was there to party and say goodbye. There was food, drinks, music, dancing and laughter. Everyone had a great time. It was the perfect way to end the club's story.

Towards the end of the party, Karen called for everyone's attention.

'I don't know what to say. Thanks so much to all of you for coming. We're really sorry this has to end.' Her voice cracked. She looked around the room and saw people who she cared about deeply, people who'd truly been on a life-changing journey with God. 'This group has been amazing, but it's time for all of us to move on. This doesn't mean we don't care about you. We really do. But we've taken this as far as it will go. I know God's got bigger and better plans for us. We might not be able to see what his plans are right now, but if we trust him, I know he'll show us. I know a lot of you are disappointed about all this. Some of you have told me you're really upset and confused. And that's OK. It's always hard to understand why something good has to end. But let's choose to remember the good times. Let's celebrate them. And let's keep close to God and follow where he leads us next.'

The most difficult thing about the end of the club was the uncertainty. For many of the club members, the future wasn't clear. How many of them would fit into church? How easy would they each find it to keep going with God? Karen had no choice but to trust God with their future. It was time for the next step for them. It dawned on Karen how much God had taught her through running the club. She realized that the club had forced her to grow up, confront her own past, and learn to rely on God more and more. But now it was time for the next step for her, too. God had changed all of them through the youth club. But it was time for the next step now. It was time for a new start.

Commentary

It's always hard when something good comes to an end. It's even harder when it's something that God has been involved in very powerfully. Everyone in this youth club struggled with the idea of the club ending. The young people themselves felt insecure, disappointed and vulnerable. The club leaders worried that the next step for the young people was unclear; that there was nothing they could do to make sure they stayed close to God. The challenge for all of them was to entrust themselves and each other to God.

In Acts 1, we find Jesus' disciples dealing with similar feelings. The previous three years with Jesus had been incredible, a barrage of surprises, miracles and lessons to learn. There had been crippling lows: rejection, failure, and the darkest hour of all, Jesus' death. There had been unbelievable highs:

healings, miracles, life-changing teaching, and Jesus' staggering resurrection. Being with Jesus had transformed the disciples' lives beyond recognition. But now it was time for it all to end. Suddenly, apparently without warning, Jesus was taken into heaven, and the disciples were left alone.

How must the disciples have been feeling at this point? It's no stretch to assume they were feeling much the same way as the young people from the closing youth club. Perhaps they felt confused and let down. Certainly they would have felt disappointed. More than likely, they would have felt fear and uncertainty about the future. All they had to hold onto was Jesus' promise that he would send the Holy Spirit, and that in this way he truly would be with them always. For the disciples, the future was unclear. All they could do was celebrate what had gone before, and trust God for the next step. And in the end, God's plan turned out to be perfect. John Stott comments:

> [Jesus] finished the work of atonement, yet that end was also a beginning. For after his resurrection, ascension and gift of the Spirit he continued his work, first and foremost through the unique foundation ministry of his chosen apostles and subsequently through the post-apostolic church of every period and place.[16]

Sometimes it's right for a good thing to end. Even a God-centred group with a fantastic history sometimes has to come to an end in order for the next step in God's plan to be possible. Sometimes something great has to end in order for something even better to start. At times like these, we simply have to entrust ourselves and each other to God, even when his plan isn't clear. A wise person once said: 'I don't know what the future holds, but I know who holds the future.'

Think about...

- How do you know when it's right for a group to end?
- When this happens, how can you celebrate what God has done through the group?
- How easy do you find it to trust God with the future of people you care about?

Chapter 8

Expectations

'You're not playing football here!' the old lady barked at the three young teenagers kicking a foam ball around the church car park. No one was being hurt and the soft ball would hardly cause lasting damage to a car, yet that was not the point. She was not prepared to tolerate these 'young upstarts' taking over the church's land on a Sunday lunchtime. This was not a place for fun and recreation – it was holy ground. The lads picked up their ball and left the car park, feeling angry and muttering curses under their breath. This was not the first time that Barbara had needed to keep some younger people in line. There was the time she had instructively pointed out that baseball caps were not appropriate in church, and the occasion when she had helpfully reminded two young lads – three weeks running – not to skateboard in or around the church steps. And there was the time when she had noticed a fresh tattoo on another lad's arm and felt compelled to say that if people must inflict such 'art' upon their bodies, then they should at least have the decency to keep it covered up during church.

Barbara was not alone. The vast majority of the congregation was very set in its ways. Church must be done in a certain manner and this manner was certainly not to be interfered with. The vast church building that cut into the urban landscape resembled a monument to a bygone age in every detail. Ruled by religiosity, this place seemed to operate as if wearing the right clothes and acting the right way – sticking to a set of rules – was what being a Christian meant. In order to be seen as godly and upright, certain conduct was essential for church members. If you could reel off Old Testament facts, names and stories by rote, then you were OK. Prizes were handed out to children who could list the longest biblical genealogies in full, though no such prize was given for articulating the gospel.

If you went along with the church's eclectic mix of morality, then that was fine; you didn't stand out. The problem with this was the complex mesh of anomalies found within their moral framework. Some unimportant issues were blown out of all proportion, whilst other moral dilemmas were left unaddressed and brushed under the carpet. In a four- or five-year period there seemed to be very little teaching on morality, yet any new church member had to learn to navigate their way around a strange collection of ideals expressed within the congregation. If you preferred to read a tabloid newspaper, then your eternal destiny was most definitely in doubt, yet if you got your girlfriend pregnant outside of marriage, most people would turn a blind eye and maintain a very British silence.

The church was full of an underlying and deep-rooted sense of duty. What really mattered was Sunday church and all the other weekly gatherings. For this community of believers, 'real' Christianity involved going to church twice on a Sunday and never missing a Bible study, prayer meeting or midweek cell group. Additionally, mandatory sign-up to every possible rota was the mark of a true, committed church member. This 'real' Christianity seemed to involve spending as many hours as possible in the church building every week.

Was this it? Was this really what Christianity was about? There was a glaring paradox in operation: a church culture where you had to conform to the pattern of behaviour required by the assembly, but in which what you did in private was your own business.

There was some 'interesting' theology as well. There was unfaltering evangelistic zeal in some of the church's views, yet these issues never really seemed worth dying over – not least the idea that women must not be involved in any kind of teaching or church leadership. In the main, the church was theologically sound and did at least believe in core doctrines like the Trinity. However, their implicit take on a Triune God was somewhat different to orthodox evangelicalism. The Trinity in this place was God the Father, God the

Son and the Holy Scriptures. There was simply no place for the Holy Spirit. This was shown in the lack of freedom the congregation felt – most notably during the dreary and drawn-out times of sung worship. Never would a sermon stray from its scripted text, never would space be given over for prophetic words to be shared, or for God to supernaturally speak life and direction into this church. Prayer was typically formulaic, and as for speaking in tongues – no chance! Any suggestion that people were missing out would be greeted with hostility. The leadership party line on the Holy Spirit was a strong and assured refrain: 'That only happens in those wacko churches. All that stuff ended at Pentecost.'

The church seemed to have decided that God's ways were clear and there was no need to expect anything unusual to happen. They were happy to believe in a Bible full of surprises and yet had created a strand of Christianity that was entirely closed to anything new. God the Father was fine, as was Jesus, but the Holy Spirit was just too unpredictable for this place. Of course, the church was happy to sing, 'When the Spirit of the Lord was within my heart I would dance as David danced', yet their attitude towards worshipful expression, and indeed how life was then lived from Monday to Saturday, seemed so different. They were too afraid to embrace the Holy Spirit and express their love for God in public worship. This didn't seem to tally up with the lyrical sentiment of their strident song selection about dancing naked before the Lord!

All respect was earned in this congregation through years of Christian living and service. While Jesus worked with the unlikely and took risks, in this church you earned your stripes firstly through the number of years you had been in attendance, and secondly through how long you had been alive. Whereas the Bible is full of examples of young people doing great things (Jeremiah was 'only a child' – see Jeremiah 1:6; Elisha was the youngest of twelve; Mary was a teenager, as were most of the disciples), in this church you were not good enough until you were old enough. Eldership meant 'oldership' and young people had to wait their turn, just as previous generations had done. It was the place of every mature member to teach these new generations true patience, stoic endurance and a godly perseverance which they could never learn from their godless, celebrity-infused, instant culture. Whereas the Bible had no real boundaries according to age, this church created them as required. Regardless of education, training and individual experiences, a young person could simply never know better than someone older.

Any constructive, creative suggestions from the youth were greeted with a patronizing smile and that wonderful mantra that trips off the tongue of some older people: 'With a bit more life experience, son, you'll grow out of your attitude and see the world for what it really is.' It was OK and perfectly acceptable for younger people in the secular world to be a cultural driving force, but 'This is church and that's not going to happen here!'

This all made the church an incredibly hard place to be young and Christian. Teenagers wouldn't always realize quite how hard it was because they never knew any different. Yet this was all about to change as a youth group for older teenagers was established. This was designed to be a place where the young people could look at issues of church, the world and Christianity more widely, more deeply and within a safe context. It was led by a couple not much older than the teenagers and was intended to be godly, yet fun; an alternative to the church services that the group went to. Rarely could the suggestions from a teenage focus group that church should 'Add some laughs' or 'Have a happy week'[17] be more aptly necessary than in this particular church community.

As this new youth group met together, things did indeed begin to change. Their previous involvement in church had always been so passive. They had never been allowed to question things before, but in this new setting, suddenly they were encouraged to explore and question things. This was illustrated in one of the early weeks when one of the leaders asked the group whether or not sex before marriage was wrong. The unanimous answer was 'Yes, it's wrong.' The leader then asked them to explain why it was wrong. At this point no one could articulate a response and it soon became clear that they didn't have a response. Their response was simply a knee-jerk reaction learnt from years of viewing the world through the lens of their congregation's worldview. Clearly, for the group leaders, there would be some work to do. Over the years, the group had been spoon-fed an eclectic collection of 'Christian' opinion without ever really hearing an explanation. Additionally, they had never before been given the opportunity to ask why things were as they were and why certain responses had been passed on to them in that way.

The group continued to meet and found within their new environment a real freedom. They discussed issues that had never been touched on in church. These discussions covered everything from homosexuality, to why wars happen, to how can I be filled with the Holy Spirit? It took a few weeks to get going, but once the young people realized that it truly was a safe environment, they quickly began to open up. The leaders made it all very inclusive. It was not 'them and us', but the whole group setting out on an explorative journey of faith together. People had questions – that was fine – but what was now important was having the new-found freedom to express opinions and explore the reasoning behind things.

Each member of the youth group was finding that their faith was strengthening as areas of it began to be deconstructed for the first time. As a group member pointed out one week, 'If Jesus truly is the Way, the Truth and the Life, why then are so many Christians too scared to question anything? Surely, all the questioning just affirms who Jesus is. That's what I'm finding, anyway.'

One of the problems that arose quickly was that the group began to be a little disheartened with the church they had grown up in. Each one of them started to realize that there was so much more out there. Their previous lack of exposure to a wider form of Christianity had meant that they were content in church. Now that they were discovering more about this Christian stuff, they were growing increasingly frustrated at the fact that their church was not experiencing all of this too. People were missing out!

In addition to meeting as a group, they socialized together, visited numerous Christian events and had even been away on Christian residentials, serving other young people. Their expectations were being transformed as to what God could do. They now believed that God could transform the world, and not just them! Their faith was growing off the scale and, naturally, they wanted to see things happen. After all, Jesus himself said, 'If you have faith as small as a mustard seed, you can say to this mulberry tree, "Be uprooted and planted in the sea," and it will obey you' (Luke 17:6). The group wanted to see mountains move in their own lives. As time drew on, each one of them experienced great change and new things of God.

There was John, for example, who had been a right rebel until God had brought him back to himself. He had tried out every hedonistic pleasure the world had to offer him, yet had only been truly fulfilled when he found Jesus. He was delighted to be a Christian and discovered that with time and freedom, his understanding of God was blown wide open. John had been at a Christian event where people were asked if they wanted to be filled with the Holy Spirit. Without knowing quite why, he leapt forward to be prayed for. As he was prayed for, John felt the presence of God come upon him incredibly powerfully and he started to laugh. At first he tried to stop the giggles but he realized that there was no reason to resist, and so he laughed and laughed. He was overwhelmed with the presence of the Holy Spirit and though he didn't fully understand it, he knew it was a good thing. This went on for over an hour and at the end of it John simply said, 'I will never be the same again.'

At the same event, Rebecca sat near the back. She was really quiet and lacking in confidence. Rebecca had always been made to go to church and had resented being dragged along week upon week by her mum. What made it worse was that mum insisted she went along dressed smartly and actually forced her to get up and join in during the singing. One night during the event they also asked if anyone wanted to become a Christian. The speaker had preached with power about the transforming message of the gospel, yet Rebecca was stunned when loads and loads of young people stood up to become Christians. She herself was deeply moved and stood to do the same. Once the evening was finished, she crumpled up in a corner and sobbed overwhelmingly because of what Jesus had done in her life. One of the group leaders came over and prayed quietly with Rebecca. This would be the most significant moment of her life. From then on, she would still be herself but with much more confidence and an increasing understanding that church was not about duty, but about a relationship with God. Jesus was her King.

Another member of the group was Colin. He had grown up in a Christian home but only realized what Christianity was all about when shown something of the Holy Spirit who was living, vibrant and real. What he experienced transformed him. Colin now wanted to live for Jesus with everything he had. Yes, there were a few things in his life that needed to be sorted out, but he had the courage to set out to change things with God's help. One of the areas of his life that needed attention was his non-Christian partner. Colin began speaking to her at length about his faith and they agreed to do an Alpha course together.

Another member of the group who was totally transformed was Phil. He was a really quiet guy who never knew anything more than his immediate environment. He loved Jesus in his own way, but by being exposed to different Christian teachings, he learnt some of what it truly meant to follow him. Phil was baptized in the Holy Spirit and was quickly transformed from a shrinking violet into a mighty man of God. He went from always being in the background to being the first to pray. He prayed for healings, for others to encounter the Holy Spirit, even revival in Britain. The list was endless. He wanted to make every moment count and became a leader of others. He went from having an inherited form of Christianity to knowing Jesus as his personal Lord and King. He went from understanding the theory of Christianity to seeing it become an everyday reality in his own life. His level of faith had been transformed and now he wanted to change the world for Jesus, living all-out for him.

Many others were changed: transformed from being shy and withdrawn in church, to speaking, leading and playing instruments at the front; from being insular to truly caring about those around them; from being caught up in a religious lifestyle of 'dos and don'ts' to being free in the Spirit. It is amazing to think of what can happen when God gets hold of a bunch of people and broadens their horizons.

It's not all easy for the group. Many of them still struggle greatly with the model of church around them. They are often still not heard because they aren't considered old enough to have a valid opinion. Some have even had to leave because God has moved them on. Yet what is so exciting is that a bunch of teenagers led that church in what it means to experience more of God than had previously been expected. We need to expect God to move in incredible and mysterious new ways. After all, he is a God who is full of surprises. Let's not confine these things to moments and movements in the Bible – God wants to do new things today as well. And it's not just for our sake, but for that of others in our churches too, and for the transformation of our immediate communities and ultimately the world. We must never allow ourselves to be a church that holds young people back just because our expectations of God differ slightly, or even greatly, from theirs.

Commentary

Jesus never intended to leave behind a predictable and methodical form of Christianity. We were not left with a simple and prescriptive structure of belief that helps us get through this life in one piece. Jesus himself never created a staid order of things, or a simple list of dos and don'ts. Instead, from Pentecost in Acts 2, we were left with the Holy Spirit in order to help us serve the King and fulfil the Great Commission. As we learn in 2 Corinthians 3:7–18, the Old Covenant was written on stones but the new one upon our hearts. Church should not be reduced to stones today. Jesus superseded this. Chafin and Ogilvie put it this way:

The religion that is based upon a list of things Christians do or don't do will usually fade into insignificant irrelevance. In a world where millions are starving each year, rules about whether it's a sin to shop for food on Sunday seem out of order. Where nations continue to use vast resources on weapons of destruction, arguing over beards or hairstyles for Christians seems irrelevant. All the little questions of 'right or wrong' which legalistic Christians have asked in the past seem to fade away like the glow on Moses' face.[18]

We need to stop being part of a legalistic church that revels in rules and is terrified of leaving its comfort zone as God does new things. As human beings, we are comfortable with clear rules and defined boundaries, but God did not create us for a simple existence, where response is robotic and devoid of passion. Instead, we are challenged to expect the unexpected and believe that God can do great and new things. Jesus himself says, just before going to heaven, that 'In my name they will drive out demons; they will speak in new tongues; they will pick up snakes with their hands; and when they drink deadly poison, it will not hurt them at all; they will place their hands on sick people, and they will get well' (Mark 16:17–18). This does not sound like the kind of Christianity we so often experience at local-church level.

It makes you wonder what it is that so many of us are afraid of. Would it really be that bad to lose control of your life and your church? After all, Jesus says, 'If anyone would come after me, he must deny himself and take up his cross and follow me. For whoever wants to save his life will lose it, but whoever loses his life for me will find it' (Matthew 16:24–25). If we are Christians, then surely our expectations and lives are all in God's hands anyway. The amazing missionary Jim Elliot, who was martyred in serving the Auca Indians, once famously said: 'He is no fool who gives what he cannot keep to gain what he cannot lose.' It's about time we started denying our human frameworks and set expectations of what God is and is not going to do, and replaced these with fresh expectations – ones in which faith really is the substance of things hoped for. No longer is life prescribed on tablets of stone. Now, in the New Covenant, the message is about our hearts.

It's not right for us to limit our expectation as to who God is and what he might do. We must no longer accept a form of safe Christianity simply because it makes us feel at home. The God of the Bible is the same today and we need to believe that he wants to do some incredible things with us now. Most of all we must believe that God wants to do great and new things amongst the emerging generations. Let's not restrict them to the experiences of church we may have had, or indeed, the limited understanding of God that we currently possess. Surely, it's hugely damaging for us to remain closed to a movement of the Spirit, even if only for the sake of new generations. Our Lord is far bigger than any set of rules, and if he needs to use a bunch of young people to show us this, then he will.

Think about...

- Are your expectations of what God can/will do great enough?
- Do you ever hold others back by conforming to a legalistic and formulaic method of Christianity?
- What might happen to your life/church/ community if the Holy Spirit came upon you in a new and dynamic way? How do you feel about this?

Chapter 9

Building Community

I'd always gone to church, for as long as I could remember. My family were Christians, so we went to church on Sundays. It was just what we did. And, at least when I was little, I mostly enjoyed it. Church meant Sunday School, and Sunday School meant games, lots of nice sugary orange squash, and some cool pictures to colour in. And lots of friends.

But as I got older, church got less fun. By the time I hit my mid-teens, church was starting to feel like a chore. No Sunday School any more. No games, no sugary orange squash, no pictures to colour in. And actually, most of my friends had disappeared too. But I was a Christian, so I went to church on Sundays. It was just what I did. Even if, by this stage, I didn't really know why.

Sunday nights meant youth group. At youth group we talked, we drank coffee, then we went home. And it didn't go much beyond that. But I was a Christian, so I went to youth group on Sunday nights. It was just what I did. To be fair, my youth group helped me a lot, but if you'd asked me why I was there, I'd probably have struggled to give you a decent answer. I didn't really know why we bothered.

I got the impression the others didn't really know why we bothered either. When we got together, we'd always sit with the people we knew best, and not really talk to anyone else. We'd have a bit of a discussion, and maybe pray, then go our separate ways and, because most of us went to different schools, we wouldn't see each other again for a week. During the school year, fewer and fewer of us would be there. Exam revision, sport fixtures and sunshine lured us away from the Sunday night gatherings. Things came to a head on one fateful Sunday night in June, when only two of us even turned up. Whatever it was we were supposed to be there for, it wasn't happening.

I can still remember the day I finally started to get it.

Clive, the youth leader, suggested a weekend away. It sounded like a good idea. A couple of days to mess about in the countryside and argue about God appealed to me. And a number of us were just finishing our exams, so this sounded like a chance to blow off some steam.

It all started quite promisingly. The venue for the weekend was a youth hostel with a big field at the back (which looked ideal for a game of touch rugby) and dormitories with bunk beds. (Of course, this prompted the inevitable scramble for the top bunks, and also, at least in the boys' dorm, the challenge of who could get around the room without touching the floor.) The hostel also had a TV, which allowed us to keep track on the tennis at Wimbledon.

After dinner on the Friday night, the leaders had a treasure hunt for us. This involved a list of questions, challenges and initiative tests, with a prize for the most successful team. All the answers, we were told, were to be found somewhere in the sleepy village just down the road. We split into teams and headed off. I teamed up with Nick, Lizzie and Rich. It soon dawned on us that this wouldn't be easy.

'"Who is the patron saint of the village?" How are we supposed to find that out?'

'"How many people live here?" What do they want us to do? Count them?'

'They want us to get a policeman's helmet. How are we supposed to do that?!'

After an hour or so of running around the village and attracting very strange looks from the locals, we headed back to the hostel for prizes, hot chocolate and bed. Of course, 'bed' didn't necessarily mean 'sleep'. In the case of the girls, it apparently meant pelting each other with items of clothing. For the boys, bedtime was a chance to sit around in the dorm, telling jokes.

'What's white and can't climb trees?'

'Dunno. What *is* white and can't climb trees?'

'A fridge.'

A splutter of laughter.

'That's the most stupid joke I've ever heard!'

'All right, you tell one, then.'

'OK. What's red and invisible?'

Silence.

'No tomatoes!'

Another silence.

'Oh, please yourselves.'

'I've got one.'

'Go on, then.'

'There's this guy who wants to get in shape, so he's looking for a gym. And he's walking through the city one day, and he passes this skyscraper with a sign outside that says, "New gym opening here today". So he goes inside. He takes the lift to the top floor, and he finds this big empty room with a woman inside, and...'

The door swung open. It was Clive.

'Keep it down, lads. It's gone midnight. You should probably think about going to sleep.'

'All right, Clive.'

'Yeah, thanks Clive. Night night.'

'Night night, fellas.'

After breakfast the next day, we did the first 'Bible' bit. We sat down, read a bit of the Bible, and talked about what it might mean. It was fun. Arguing about God has always appealed to me, and I was on a roll. About halfway through the session, a thought hit me that stopped me in my tracks. *This was exactly the same as one of our Sunday night meetings.* I looked around me. Everyone was sitting with their mates, the people they knew best. Change the surroundings from the basement room of a youth hostel to Clive's sitting room, and this would be a typical Sunday night. I thought back on what we'd done since we'd arrived the night before. The treasure hunt. I'd done it with Rich, Nick and Lizzie: my best friends in the group, the people I knew best. Dinner and breakfast: I'd sat with my mates. Watching the tennis: ditto.

Nothing was changing. We were happy in our little clusters, and this was how we were going to stay. We'd go home on Sunday evening, not see each other for the rest of the week, and get back into the same old routine. It was only a matter of time before it went back to me and one other person turning up on a Sunday evening.

I didn't say much for the rest of the session. I didn't say much during lunch (during which, we all sat in our little friendship clusters, of course). The rest of the day passed in something of a blur. But at least I had an idea now of exactly what needed to change in the group. If you'd asked me before the weekend what was wrong with the group, I'd probably have said that people just needed to be more committed – to make the effort to turn up more often. I don't think I'd have known why this was a problem. Now I thought I knew. Why bother turning up on a Sunday night, when you're comfortable with your small group of friends? What's the point of committing to a larger group, if no one in the group seems committed to you? If the group was ever going to go beyond coffee and Bible study on a Sunday, all the little friendship groups needed to open up. We all needed to let our guard down. As it turned out, the leaders had already thought of this, and they'd made plans to do something about it. God seemed to have made some plans too.

A few weeks before, Lizzie had had a phone call, inviting her to appear on a Sunday morning TV programme. (One of those sort-of-religious programmes you get on a Sunday. The kind with one or two gospel choirs, dotty old ladies talking about doing the flowers for their church and some anonymous middle-aged woman presenting it.) Lizzie didn't say how they'd got hold of her, only that they wanted her to talk about her experiences of being bullied a couple of years before.

As it happened, the Sunday when the programme was aired was the Sunday we were away at the youth hostel. So, come Sunday morning, we all settled down in front of the TV to witness Lizzie's fifteen minutes of fame. As Lizzie appeared on the screen, we cheered, excited at the novelty of seeing someone we knew on TV. But as Lizzie spoke, the atmosphere in the room changed. She described how lonely and isolated she'd felt while she was being bullied. She explained how God and her family had helped her through, and helped her to forgive the people who'd made her miserable.

At the end of the programme, we were quiet and subdued. Lizzie's willingness to make herself vulnerable had challenged us. None of us had realized what she'd been through. What kind of difference would it make to the group, if we were all willing to be that vulnerable with each other? Before lunch, we had a chance to find out.

We huddled on the grass at the back of the hostel. Each of us had a sheet of paper, and wrote our names on the top. The idea was to pass our sheets of paper around the circle, each writing something encouraging on each sheet. Anything other than physical appearance could be commented on. This couldn't be that hard, could it? Well, as it turned out, yes, it could. To tell someone else what you really think of them, and to hear what other people think of you, both require you to make yourself vulnerable. Was I imagining it, or was there a bit of tension around the circle?

When we got our own sheets back, we opened them up. We sat and read what the others really thought of us. The comments ranged from the faintly bizarre ('Good at spelling') to the highly affirming ('Leadership qualities'). The question put before us was: Did anything on our sheets surprise us? Well, yes. I'd always suspected that my friends thought I was really a bit of a plonker. Apparently this wasn't the case. (Or at least, if they did think I was a plonker, they thought I could rise above that...) This was good news. And it got me thinking. If I really did have some significant gifts, how could I use them? More to the point, how could I use them to help my friends? As different people in the group read out what had been written on their sheets of paper, something very interesting emerged. Nobody had the same gifts, the same strengths. It might sound silly, but this possibility hadn't occurred to me before. Paul was an encourager, relentlessly positive and full of faith. Nick was creative and inspiring. Sophie was patient and caring, a real pastor. We were all different, but we all complemented each other. We all needed each other. I realized that to make our group and our church strong, we all had a part to play, and we'd all be worse off if even one of us chose not to play that part.

'Anyone want another sausage?' Tony called across the field. I hesitated briefly. I'd had three hotdogs already. But if there were still some left, there was no sense wasting them. I picked up my paper plate, stood up, and made my way towards the barbeque for the fourth time. As I wandered across the field, I glanced around me at the other members of the group. Lucy, Jess and Sophie were sat on a bench, trying to whistle through their fingers, and laughing at each other's efforts. Paul was trying to impress some of the girls with his stories about Australia. Rich and Lizzie were asleep, flat on their backs on a rug. Nick was prowling between the small knots of people sat on the grass, stealing left-over food, and pretending to be a secret agent. It struck me how different some of these guys were. And most of them were fairly strange. But they all had something important to offer too.

The weekend was drawing to a close. The smoke from the barbeque was dispersing, and as the threatened rain finally began to appear, we reluctantly retreated into the basement room. I pushed the remains of my fourth hotdog into my mouth as I walked. I reflected that it had been a great weekend. It had been fun, and a good experience in itself, and I also wondered what would change in the group when we got home. We'd made ourselves vulnerable to each other and encouraged each other in a way we never had before. We'd got a clearer idea of what we could all do, and how valuable we all were to the group and the church. Surely the group would be stronger from now on. And we could build on this to make the group more open to newcomers. But perhaps I was starting to get ahead of myself. For now, I was just happy to enjoy being part of a group where I felt I belonged.

Once we were in the basement, we sat in a circle. The only sound was the rain beating on the windows. Clive read some words from 1 Corinthians. He broke a loaf of bread in half and encouraged us all to take some bread, eat it, and remember Jesus. As I looked at the faces of the people around me, I knew that I didn't completely understand all of them. But I also knew that I needed them. I couldn't escape the fact that we were a team, one body. And as I realized this, I also realized that Jesus was there in that room with us.

Commentary

In Luke 24, we find two of Jesus' followers on a journey together. They are confused and hurt by what has gone before, not understanding why Jesus had to die, and not quite believing that he truly has come back to life. I wonder if their friendship is strengthened by the time they spend together, being open with one another and sharing their struggles and disappointments. Moreover, as they open up to one another, Jesus walks with them. It's intriguing to note that the two disciples don't recognize Jesus at first. And yet, they still seem to be willing to trust him, and welcome him to join them on their journey. In being willing to accept and welcome a stranger, they in fact welcome Jesus.

In the story above, a group of young people have a similar experience. They all have their own struggles, disappointments and insecurities. But they begin to open up, make themselves vulnerable to each other, and begin to share their struggles. When this happens, they find they become closer as a group, and begin to appreciate each other more. And as they choose to accept each other, regardless of how strange they appear to each other, they welcome Jesus among them and experience his presence.

As the disciples on the way to Emmaus discuss what has happened, and try to make sense of it all, Jesus speaks to them. As they try to understand the Scriptures, Jesus brings clarity. And, perhaps most profoundly, as the disciples eat together, their eyes are opened and they recognize him (see Luke 24:31). The parallels between this scene and the Last Supper are striking (see Luke 22:19), and it's indisputable that echoing the Last Supper by taking communion remains an intensely powerful way to come face to face with Jesus. However, I believe, as Wiersbe does, that this scene from the Emmaus story has implications which reach further than the communion service.[19]

The mere act of eating together with friends, giving thanks to God, can be an opportunity to recognize Jesus and experience his presence. The ancient Jewish culture prized hospitality. To share a meal with someone was to make it absolutely clear that you accepted them and welcomed them. Hence the Pharisees' horror that Jesus eats with 'sinners' (Luke 15:2).[20] This also goes some way to explaining why Jesus refers to heaven as a 'feast', a huge celebration meal (Matthew 8:11). There is still something uniquely powerful about sharing a meal with someone, even 2,000 years later and in a different culture. For a group of people to share a meal still signals mutual respect and acceptance. For the young people at the youth hostel, both the ritual to remember Jesus' sacrifice, and the barbeque which went before, were opportunities to enjoy one another's company, reflect on the unity and diversity of the group, and acknowledge that Jesus was among them. Perhaps simply encouraging a group of people to share a meal is a significant step towards building a sense of community in the group. Perhaps it even offers them a small glimpse of the Kingdom of God.

And finally for the two disciples, their encounter with Jesus inspires them to share their story with others. They return to Jerusalem, find the eleven, and tell them what Jesus said and did while he was with them. For the modern youth group we've just seen, their encounter with Jesus and their new-found unity inspired them in a similar way. A few months after the end of this story, they started a monthly youth event to tell their friends the difference Jesus had made in their lives.

Building a sense of community is absolutely crucial for a healthy youth group or indeed a healthy church. The presence of God is so much clearer in a strong community. And it's only once a group feel secure, accepted and valued that they will be confident to invite others into the group. So we must do whatever we can to foster strong and meaningful relationships within our churches, and support and accept one another. From this foundation, we may find it easier and more natural to share what Jesus has done for us with our friends.

T h i n k   a b o u t ...

- What can you do to show other people in your church that you accept and welcome them?
- What opportunities do you and your friends have to share experiences you are going through, whether positive or negative?
- Do you ever share a meal with your church, your housegroup or your circle of friends?

Chapter 10

Failure

What an amazing opportunity this young and gregarious bunch of teenagers had been given. In the middle of a difficult council estate sat a potential beacon of light and hope – a dilapidated building that would soon be restored to its resplendent glory of yesteryear. After years of praying for such a lifeline to arise, the unused community hall was now theirs to use however they deemed fit. No need to keep bleating on to the adults in the church about format and style of services. They now had their own church building and they knew that they would certainly make the most of this opportunity. To try and keep things a little on track, there were a few youth leaders a generation or so older than the young people, but all in all, the new dawn had begun. This bunch of enthusiastic teenagers were going to do things their own way.

Forget the old arguments over adult attendees' disdain for drums in worship. These guys were going to have a DJ leading God's praise from his decks. Additionally, the host would hold a microphone and spend his evening whipping the baying crowd into a frenzy through his MCing. If there was going to be a preacher, then it would be a cool one who didn't just talk at you for ages. No need for a vicar in a dog collar – any speaker in this new church would have to wear jeans and no ties were allowed! People could come as they felt comfortable and no comment would be made. None of this dressing up funny on a Sunday malarkey – this was to be church done in a casual style.

Church needn't always start on time. They would meet from 7:30 p.m., but if the crowd weren't ready or there yet, they would start later. It was not some formal exam, but instead a gathering of like-minded people that would be far more chilled out than conventional Christian gatherings. It wouldn't have to be as polite as other churches either. If you needed the loo during the service, then you'd just go. If the speaker said something you disagreed with, then there was no need to be submissive and quiet. Any speaker would have to be prepared to encounter questions and interaction from the floor. This new format for church was going to be so radically different and yet at the same time, relaxed. No waiting till the end of church for a cup of coffee. You could have one as the service went along. This bunch of young people genuinely believed that they would change the shape and face of church forever.

Amidst all the dreaming and aspirational thinking, the reality soon dawned that this all had to start somewhere. In order to change the whole landscape of church for the entire Western world, they would have to begin somewhat more humbly. After all, some old guy had been preaching just the week before that God always does in the small what later he will do in the big. He'd preached that, in order to see God do unbelievable things, often we had to put in a massive effort and be willing to see God change the small things first.

The young people had to start somewhere and so they began by getting their paintbrushes out. They arrived *en masse* at their new building with their varied selection of brushes, tools and paint gathered from their parents' sheds. They pooled their resources and took great delight in setting about their task. Step one was stripping the horrible woodchip wallpaper from the walls and then filling in any holes. This painstaking task seemed to take forever, but their continued persistence meant that they finished it in the end.

Then it was time to paint. The grey walls came to life in resplendent purple and the group took great delight in seeing this transformation. As they painted their new worship house, there was a great amount of adrenaline and enthusiasm flowing throughout the group. The new appearance of the hall was symbolic of the fact that things would be different from now on. A generous philanthropist had donated a large sum of money, which meant that little expense need be spared. As well as paint, cash was spent on funky furniture. Since this was a little before the Swedish monopoly on functional furniture had conquered the globe, this process took the youth group a fair while as the young people trawled local shops and trendy markets for just the right look. Each bit of furniture and decoration needed to be perfect. This was their stamp they were putting on the building.

The lighting in the new building had to be subtle and contemplative, and so instead of any lights being on the ceiling, all illumination came from uplighters in the four corners of the room, with a tasteful scattering of lava lamps. In a previous age the lights would have been on the ceiling, but here it was covered alternatively with a collection of tie-dyed sheets. The whole place was designed to look more like a trendy nightclub than a church building. The group owned this style. As they looked upon their creation, they echoed God's thoughts towards his own. They 'saw that it was good'.

After months of preparation, the building was finally ready to be opened. Amidst much DJ fanfare, with music blaring out from the liberally spread speakers controlled from behind the decks, the venue was declared officially open. This was to be the start of something incredible. The collection of teenagers were convinced that now that their 'house was in order', the revival would come. After all, this was a difficult urban community and such a facility as the one they had created would be an answer to a whole plethora of sociological issues. Young people who had previously had nowhere to go would be able to join them in their new haven of chilled but godly peace. Those who would get into all kinds of trouble need no longer worry, as there was now a place to go. There was no point in going after sex, drugs and rock'n'roll on the local streets when you could go to church instead!

The honeymoon period was a wonderful time. The venue was greeted with unbridled joy by many local residents and as a solution to so much of the antisocial behaviour caused by teenagers on the estate. The local police praised what was being done and cited the new church building as a key component in reducing the levels of crime in the area. Local media became interested and the newspaper ran a centre-page spread on what was being done, with loads of photos. Even the local radio interviewed a number of young people about the new church. All of this initial success was being enjoyed by everyone. It seemed that every area of the project was going well. Quickly, the size of the group attending grew as previous attendance figures of around the fifteen mark soon smashed through the sixty barrier. Those who were going said it was the most dynamic, exciting and relevant church they had ever been to. This fresh brand of contemporary Christianity really scratched where people were itching and offered young people a relationship with Jesus on their own terms.

Initially the group had started meeting just once

a week, but soon demand was at such a level that this grew to twice. As a result, a new outreach strategy was birthed that seemed unstoppable: one of these meetings would be to allow Christians to grow in their faith and the other would be a social night facilitating a way into church for those who found themselves on the periphery. The success of all of this seemed to be strongly endorsed by yet more growth. From every possible angle, it appeared that everything was going so very well. After all, young people vote with their feet, don't they?

As time went on, one or two initial cracks began to appear in the middle of this fairy-tale youth congregation. Like the little cracks that first appear in fresh plaster, bit by bit things seemed less and less rosy. The first problem was the girl who got pregnant. Surely it wasn't the youth leaders' place to judge, but wasn't sex before marriage wrong? Then there were the lads caught smoking pot. What should be done about them? But this was all so small and easy to deal with compared with how to 'pastor' the guy who came out as gay. This young lad didn't see a moral problem with practising homosexuality, yet his parents were in church leadership. What on earth should the youth leaders do? There was a growing band within the youth church who were increasingly anarchic and anti any of the rules that this Christian thing seemed to throw at them.

But at the same time there was another group

emerging. These were the 'holier than thous' who had decided exactly how to live correctly and thought that those of moral disrepute were simply ignorant of what was truly holy. This troop of triumphalistic young Pharisees made it known to everyone that they were good at personal devotions, they led Christian Unions at their schools, and they never missed an opportunity to visibly outdo one another in the cause of who could be the best Christian. They could always be seen at the front of any worship service, singing the loudest, with arms aloft, always responding to calls at the front to do more, and forever volunteering for things in order to outdo their contemporaries in a bizarre form of competitive Christianity.

These young devotees did everything to express their superior brand of Christianity to the rest of the group. Any sin from other young people would be greeted with a tut and a condescending look. Any suggestion that the world was more important to them than God would be dismissed in an instant. They were, in their own words, 'single for the gospel', committed to not being in a relationship unless the Lord himself deemed it right for them. Every area of their lives seemed committed to holiness, but beneath the surface it was really only about legalism. With two such distinct groups forming within this new youth church, there were the beginnings of the perfect recipe for disaster.

With such a swiftly growing chasm forming

between the anarchists and the Pharisees, what were the leaders to do? Somewhat inevitably, they did what most humans do in similar situations: they took the easy option. They affirmed everything about the group of Christian devotees and slammed all there was to criticize in the others. One group was told how proud God was of them, and the other group was left to hang out together, with no significant adult input or interest in getting 'in' amongst those perceived as being troublemakers. Simply put, one group were groomed as the next generation of church leaders and the other were told to stay out of prison. Over the weeks and months ahead, the split within the youth group became firmly established. On one side were the 'good' teenagers with their leaders, and on the other side was anyone who was even mildly nonconformist.

Over time, the intensity of what was going on in the youth group built to a crescendo. There were problems between the factions, and even within the group of 'holy kids' things started to go wrong when one of them turned out to be a drug dealer! Despite the huge investment that had been put into this youth group, it was beginning to fall apart. The dream of what could be was turning into a nightmare. Young people were leaving in their droves as the polarity of being either a 'great Christian' or a 'shunned outcast' became more pronounced by the week. Within the non-conformist group there was a friendship circle of around twenty. Sadly, all of them left the youth church within ten months of each other. Today, not much more than ten years later, only one of them has returned to church and would make any kind of claim to follow Jesus. The others have been so burnt by what they experienced as church, that they can't even be indifferent towards it – they hate church. What incredible spiritual damage!

A whole generation of young nonconformists were lost from this experimental youth church. And what of the conformists? Well, for the next generation of supposed leaders, they didn't fare too well. At least half of them don't go to church regularly and only one or two have decided to enter into church ministry. For all of their grand spiritual statements, gestures and perceived devotional life, lasting fruit was minimal. Four years after this dream building had been opened, one of the youth workers now stood there nailing a couple of thick planks of wood across the front doors. It was no longer needed as a church. So much for changing the face and shape of church forever! The dream was over.

Commentary

As a church, we have real trouble engaging with those who rebel against the system. We try to nullify them and if this doesn't work, we seem lost as to what to do.

However, the most difficult teenager in your church is arguably the leader with the greatest potential for the future. After all, if you kick against the church as a teenager, just think how you could kick against the world in the name of Jesus as an adult! We need to start getting in amongst the teenagers in our churches and communities, paying special attention to those who are deemed 'a bit difficult'. The former head of the Evangelical Alliance and Principal of the London School of Theology, the late Gilbert Kirby, once asked why it was that God so often used the rebels. We need to keep these kind of characters in order for them to be used mightily in the service of God.

We hear so many stories of how it has gone wrong in our churches and how young people have left in their droves. At the same time, we can be so bad at acknowledging when things have actually gone well or others have really moved on in God. It's almost as if we say to ourselves, 'Well, if we don't get a 100 per cent success rate in our youth work, then we must be dramatically failing.' Yes, there are some terrible stories of failure like the one described above, but there are also times when all we choose to see is failure, even though there is great success as well.

If we look at Jesus and his disciples, there aren't many of us who would accuse him of being a failure. How dare we suggest that anyone who had hung out with Jesus as part of his close group of followers would do anything but follow him with everything they had? After all, it is surely impossible for anyone to turn away from the Son of God? However, of Jesus' youth group of twelve disciples, one of them denied Jesus (Peter: John 18:15, 25–27); one doubted him (Thomas: John 20:24–30); and one betrayed him (Judas: John 18:1–11). It is an incredible reality that in the case of the Lord himself, only 75 per cent of his disciples stayed loyal and faithful to him. This does not for one moment mean that we should adopt a blasé attitude, but rather, it should help to move us away from the self-analytical processes we go through when things seem to be going wrong. The parable of the lost sheep (Luke 15:1–7) shows us that each and every individual is worth fighting for, and we must choose to do the same. However, we won't succeed every time. Nor should we expect to do so.

The true test is not in whether or not we fail but in how we respond to failure. When Jesus reinstates Peter (John 21:15–25), an incredible truth is realized. He is the God of the second, tenth or one hundredth chance. The Bible can be very encouraging here. It is full of people who have failed God and yet are still used amazingly: Noah planted his own vineyard and got drunk on the wine he had made; Abraham was too old; Jacob was a liar; Rahab was a prostitute; David had an affair and was a murderer; Jonah ran from God; the disciples fell asleep while praying; the Samaritan woman was divorced – more than once; and Lazarus – well, Lazarus was dead! Based on this list, you could almost build up a theological position that you have to really fail in order to be used by God. This is greatly encouraging for all of us, as in our times of failure God can prove to be always faithful and stronger than our situations. As my wife so often points out when something has gone well in my ministry, 'It just goes to show that Jesus still rides on donkeys today.' Our God has a funny sense of humour, and this means that he often uses the unlikely characters, loves working with failures and delights in giving them another chance to once again serve him with a glad heart.

We must allow people to have new opportunities and be shown grace in order that they can return and not be unnecessarily lost, whilst ourselves learning from personal failings and accepting God's grace. Failure must never go by unnoticed, yet equally, we must not allow failure to overshadow the good that God has been doing through us, perhaps choosing instead to relegate ourselves to a position from which we may never recover. It is impossible for us to even hope to achieve a 100 per cent success rate in the ministries God gives us, so in our sinful humanity we must not expect perfection. From time to time, when we feel we have failed, we need to approach the God of grace in humility and allow him to dust us down, help us back up and give us the chance to start again.

T h i n k   a b o u t ...

- How do you personally respond to failure?
- What does God think about the areas in which you have failed? Do you need to allow him to show you today that he is the God of the second chance?
- Think about someone you have known who the church has failed. Write their name down and put it in your wallet or purse or somewhere else you will see it regularly. Commit to praying for this person, that God might break through into their life afresh.

Chapter 11

Forgiveness

The buzz of chatter in the hall stopped dead. Anna stood and hesitated in the doorway. She could feel the eyes of the other girls running over her, noticing her cuts and bruises. It had been over a week since it had happened, and it was clear that everyone had heard about it. Anna saw Alison and Susie, standing together on the opposite side of the hall. They were looking straight at her, but their expressions were giving nothing away. Were they feeling guilty? Satisfied? Proud, even? Anna looked away and slowly made her way towards a group of girls on her left.

Alison and Susie had told Helen about Saturday just two days after it had happened. They were sure Helen would see things their way. After all, Helen was a leader. She was used to dealing with troublemakers. If you're in the right, whatever you do to someone who crosses you is justified, isn't it? And if you don't do something about a troublemaker, doesn't that make you weak? Helen was a leader. Helen was strong.

She'd back them up. To their surprise, Helen didn't back them up. In fact, she was angry. She took them to one side to talk to them.

'Are you really proud of yourselves?! Well, I'm not proud of you. Can't you see that what you've done is wrong? Do you really think this is the way God wants us to sort out our differences? You need to say sorry to Anna.'

The two girls were confused. Everyone else had been telling them they were in the right. But now Helen was telling them something completely different. What were they supposed to do now?

Alison and Susie had been best friends for years. Everyone knew that. They went to school together, they hung out together, they got in trouble together. But then Anna turned up and things started to change. Anna was new to the group and she was trying to make friends. She was trying to make friends with Alison. After a week or two, Susie started to feel uncomfortable. She'd been best friends with Alison for years, but Anna was trying to take that away from her. Anna was trying to get her out of the way so that she could be Alison's best friend instead. What right did she have to do that?

Anna was enjoying making new friends. All the girls in the group seemed really nice, especially Alison. Alison was, well... cool. She was pretty, she always dressed well, and she was smart, too. She tested boundaries, but she knew exactly how much she could get away with before she got into trouble. No wonder Alison was popular. All the other girls wanted to be like her. But Susie wasn't so nice. She was cold. And it wasn't long before Anna realized that Susie didn't like her at all.

Alison was intrigued when Anna joined the group. She wanted to find out who Anna was and what made her tick. As Alison got to know Anna, she realized that Anna liked her and wanted to be her friend. Alison was pleased. It made her feel good to know that people wanted to be friends with her. Susie certainly did, and now Anna did. Alison wondered who wanted to be her friend the most. She decided to find out. Anyone could tell that Susie and Anna didn't like each other. It would just take a few comments here and there to get the two of them fighting to be her best friend. This would be fun. Slowly but surely, Alison began to turn Anna and Susie against each other.

Over the next few weeks, the tension between the three girls grew and grew. It had a real effect on the rest of the group too. When they got together, the atmosphere changed when one of the three walked into the room. Even the dance they were practising wasn't fun any more, because Anna and Susie could hardly stand being in the same room as each other. The girls could all see what was going on, and of course, they all had an opinion on it. Some felt sorry for Anna. All Anna was doing was trying to make some friends, trying to fit into the group. Other girls took Susie's side. Anna should have got the message that Susie and Alison were best friends. Why couldn't Anna just back off? All this tension was her fault.

Finally, the situation came to a head. One Saturday afternoon, some of the girls went out to the park together. It was a sunny day, and they reckoned there would be boys there. Anna went, partly for the boys, but mostly to spend some time with her new friends. Susie went, partly for the boys, but mostly to show Anna that she was Alison's best friend and there was nothing Anna could do about it. Alison went to make some sparks fly between Anna and Susie. And if there were boys there too, what a great audience for the face-off. The boys would think she was great.

Sure enough, as the girls arrived in the park, they spotted a gang of boys hanging around by the swings. Alison smiled and started walking towards them. The others went with her. The boys nudged each other and grinned as they saw the girls coming.

'All right, girls?'

Amidst the giggling, flirting and showing off that followed, the icy silence between Susie and Anna still couldn't be ignored.

'What's wrong with those two?' one of the boys asked.

'She thinks she's so cool,' said Susie, sneering at Anna, 'and she just can't see that nobody likes her.'

Alison turned to Anna. 'Are you going to take that?'

'Shut up!' Anna shouted at Susie. 'You're just jealous. And you're an ugly cow.'

'Why don't you get lost?' Susie yelled back. 'Nobody wants you here.'

'Yeah,' Alison chimed in, 'you're always just hanging around. It's pathetic.'

'Shut up!' Anna shouted again.

'Stupid cow.' Susie spat. For a few seconds there was an uneasy silence. Susie and Anna stood face to face, glaring at each other.

'Why don't you two just fight?' suggested a boy standing behind Anna.

'Yeah, fight it out!'

The chant went up: 'Fight! Fight! Fight!'

Smack. Anna felt her cheek stinging and her eye starting to water. She launched herself at Susie, clawing at her face and pulling her hair. Quickly, the two girls disappeared into a shrieking mess of flailing hands and feet; pushing, slapping and scratching at each other. As they tore into each other, they were aware of a circle of spectators forming around them; shouting, cheering and laughing. Anna caught sight of one of the girls recording the whole thing on her mobile phone. The next thing Anna knew, she was on her back, on the ground. As Alison stood over her, Anna realized that it had been Alison who had pushed her over. Anna screamed in pain as she felt a kick hit her in the ribs. Then another, and another, as Susie and Alison teamed up and started to pummel her. Someone else was joining in – maybe two or three other people, punching and kicking her – but Anna couldn't tell how many for sure. All she could do was wrap her arms around her head, curl her knees up to her chest, and pray for it all to end.

'Look! There's blood!'

The boys had seen enough. What had started as a bit of fun for them was getting alarming. Seeing two girls roughing each other up had been entertaining, but now it looked as though Anna might get seriously hurt. They waded in, pulling the girls off Anna and dragging them away.

'All right, that's enough.'

'She's hurt! Come on, get away.'

Slowly, Anna got to her feet, clutching her ribs and with her nose bleeding. She looked at the crowd around her, then wordlessly turned and limped away.

'She had it coming to her,' Susie announced defiantly.

'Yeah,' Alison agreed, 'we did what we had to. She was out of order.'

The girls went home to a huge amount of trouble. The next two days were a flurry of tellings-off, groundings, threats and confiscation of pocket money. Anna's mum was probably more angry and upset than anyone else. She was all for pressing charges against Alison and Susie, and she told Helen so when she met her in the street.

Susie and Alison were confused. To begin with they'd felt proud of what they'd done. Anna had been causing trouble and they'd dealt with her. And even though their parents shouted at them for going too far, they still felt they were on their side. But maybe Helen was right. Maybe saying sorry was the way to sort this all out. And Susie in particular couldn't escape the nagging feeling that this was the way God wanted them to deal with it. So, should they listen to their friends and stand their ground now, or listen to Helen and apologize to Anna?

Susie decided to find Anna and talk it over. She'd only seen Anna once since the afternoon in the park and neither of them had spoken to each other then. She decided to go round to Anna's house and find her. She strode up to the front door and rang the bell. Anna's mum answered it.

'You?! What do you want?'

'I want to talk to Anna. I...'

'Talk to Anna? You've got a nerve, after what you did to her. Get lost!'

'But...'

'I said go! We don't want your sort around here.' And she slammed the door.

This made Susie's mind up for her. So much for saying sorry. Anna was too high and mighty even to talk to her. All she'd got from being willing to say sorry was a mouthful of abuse. She and Alison had been right the first time. They should just stand their ground. They were in the right.

It didn't occur to Susie that the reason why Anna didn't want to talk to her, and the reason why Anna hadn't been around lately, was that she was terrified of another fight. She'd hardly left the house since the fight in the park, except to go to school. Something in Anna knew she had to forgive Susie and Alison for what they'd done, but how was she supposed to forgive them when they were likely to do the same thing to her again the next time she saw them? The next time she saw them, she'd be ready for them. If they wanted a fight, they'd get one.

As it turned out, the next time Anna and Susie met was only a couple of days later. Anna was walking down the High Street with two friends towards school. Susie was coming towards her. Anna saw Susie first.

'Get out of my way, you stupid tart!'

'Shut up, you stuck-up cow!'

'What's your problem?'

'You're my problem. Get out of my face!'

The two girls flew at each other, grabbing each other's hair and scratching at each other's faces. Anna's friends stepped in and dragged her away, and the girls continued on their way, yelling insults at each other as they went.

That evening, when Anna arrived at the church,

she was relieved to find that Alison and Susie weren't there. Perhaps they'd realized nobody wanted them there and decided to leave the group. As Anna talked to the other girls, she started to relax. But after a few minutes, Anna noticed that the girls she was talking to were looking past her towards the door. She turned slowly. Sure enough, there were Susie and Alison. They paused, stared at her, then looked away and started talking together. Anna's face fell. The mood in the room changed noticeably. The girls still talked, but the conversation became stilted. There was still an occasional laugh, but it sounded forced. When someone knocked over a can of Coke, instead of laughs and gentle teasing, it was greeted with silence.

Helen and the other leaders noticed. They felt the tension in the room, and they knew where it had come from. They also knew that something had to be done, before the cracks in the group became so deep they couldn't be repaired. At the end of the evening, after the games and the dance rehearsal, Helen called the girls together for the usual group discussion. She talked for a few minutes about teamwork, then asked the girls to discuss what made a good team. They came up with some good answers:

'Supporting each other.'
'Everyone doing their part.'
'Encouragement.'
'Working in harmony.'

'Right!' said Helen, decisively, 'great answers. But how good do you think we are at being a team at the moment?' There was an awkward pause. 'Not great, huh?'

Nobody said anything. One or two shook their heads slightly.

'OK,' Helen persevered, 'so what do you think God would say about that?'

'That... we need to work in harmony?' Susie suggested.

'Maybe,' Helen nodded. 'Why don't we go away and think about it?' She finished the evening by praying a simple prayer; that God would help the group be a real team and work in harmony. Afterwards, the girls began to make their way out and head for home. Helen caught Alison and Susie on the way out.

'So what do you think, then?'

'About what?' Alison asked, blankly.

'What do you think God would say about how you and Anna are getting on?'

'Well... I suppose he'd want us to say sorry...' Susie conceded.

'OK...'

'But we're in the right here. We're not going to say sorry if we're in the right,' Alison retorted.

'It's not about who's right or wrong!' Helen exclaimed. 'You know God wants us to be a team, to work in harmony. Well, we need to be willing to say sorry, if that's going to happen.'

'We'll think about it.' The two girls left, seeming unsure, but slightly less defiant than before.

The next two weeks continued in much the same way. Whenever Anna met Susie or Alison in the street, it always ended up with them rowing at best, and coming to blows at worst. The animosity between them carried on spilling over into the Monday night meetings, too. All the girls seemed wary and subdued, and the more vocal girls in the group soon turned on Anna. Weeks before, Anna and Alison had been paired together in a dance routine the girls were working on. This was now a problem.

'I'm not dancing with *her*,' Alison said with disgust. Reluctantly, she gave in to the leaders, who insisted that the girls stay in the same pairs. But for the whole practice, Alison was making comments about Anna under her breath and behaving as though she was dancing with someone who hadn't washed for several weeks. At the end of the practice, Helen took Alison to one side.

'Your behaviour has been completely unacceptable tonight, Alison. Behave like that again, and you're out. Do you understand?'

By this stage, it wasn't just Alison and Susie who were against Anna. Alison's other friends were turning on Anna too. They talked about her behind her back and giggled when she turned in their direction. They muttered insults at her when they thought nobody else could hear. They turned their backs on her when she tried to talk to them. Anna was becoming a victim and gradually she just lost the energy to fight against it. Fortunately, the other girls in the group had noticed, and they decided to do something about it. They made the effort to talk to her and make her feel included. And when Jenny overheard Alison and Susie bad-mouthing Anna, she told her straight: 'Don't listen to them. You don't need them. You've got us now, and we won't let them do this to you.'

Anna felt better. She felt more included. She felt that she now had real friends in the group. She felt safe. But although Anna was happier, this presented a new threat to the group. It seemed that everyone had now taken a side: Alison, Susie and their friends, versus Anna and her friends. The group had split in two. How long would it be before the two sides turned against each other? Helen made a difficult decision. Despite the leaders' repeated pleas to sort the situation out, despite their ongoing prayers for God to bring the girls together, Alison, Susie and Anna were no closer to being on speaking terms again. Formal mediation seemed the only solution. Helen would have to get Alison, Susie and Anna together, sit with them and go through a long and difficult process of mediation. Her heart sank at the prospect, but she knew something had to be done and she couldn't see an alternative. There was no time to fit in the mediation for at least a week, though. And in the meantime, there was a sleepover planned for the weekend. Twelve hours with Anna, Susie and Alison in the same building. This could be a disaster.

On Friday night, Anna's mum brought her to the sleepover. If Alison and Susie were there, she had decided to bring Anna home straight away. But there was no sign of Alison and Susie, so Anna stayed. Helen spoke to Anna's mum, to reassure her that the leaders were looking out for Anna and wouldn't accept any kind of bullying. Anna's mum seemed satisfied and went home. Perhaps this would all work out OK after all.

Within half an hour, Susie and Alison turned up. This had the potential to be a nightmare. The tension in the group couldn't be allowed to go on.

'Any comments, any horrible behaviour, and you're going straight home, OK?'

'OK,' Susie and Alison agreed.

'You're going to be nice to Anna tonight, right?'

'Yeah, all *right*,' Alison replied, with some exasperation. Helen wondered whether she meant it.

The dance performance wasn't far away. The girls decided to take this opportunity for an extra rehearsal. They got together in the hall and started the music. They began going through the steps, tensely, perhaps a little stiffly, but with purpose. Here at least, it seemed they were beginning to work in harmony. Helen watched with a small sense of relief. But then, suddenly, a thump as a body hit the floor. Jane had spun around, according to the steps, but then tripped over her own foot and fell over. For a second there was silence. Then someone started giggling. The giggling spread. Soon everyone was giggling. The girls tried to continue the routine, but by now they were laughing so much, they just couldn't do it.

Helen smiled and suggested taking a break. The girls agreed, and sat down for a drink and a chat. After a few minutes, Helen noticed that Alison, Susie and Anna were all missing. Was this a good or bad sign? She decided to check. Helen checked the most likely places first – the toilets, the kitchen, round the back of the building – but the three girls were nowhere to be seen. Where were they? A slow, creeping sense of dread started to come over Helen as she began to imagine where the girls might be, and what Alison and Susie might be doing to Anna. What would Anna's mum say if she was here now, after the promises Helen had made about looking after Anna? Just as Helen was beginning to get really worried, she heard low voices from a side room, next to the hall. As she opened the door, she found Alison, Anna and Susie, sitting together and talking. They looked up as she came in.

To Helen's amazement, the three girls were sitting facing each other, holding hands. There were tears in their eyes.

'It's OK, Helen,' Susie said quietly, 'we've said sorry. We've all forgiven each other.'

Helen was speechless.

'Like you said,' Alison explained, 'this is what God would want us to do.'

The girls stood up and wordlessly swooped into a three-way hug.

As the three of them emerged from the room, everyone realized something major had changed. All three of them seemed incredibly peaceful. As Alison, Anna and Susie explained what had happened, that sense of peace began to spread to every other girl in the hall. From that point on, the group was never the same again. They'd seen an impossible situation completely turned around. They'd seen fierce enemies become friends. They'd learned to work in harmony after all. And all it took was a little forgiveness.

Commentary

Anna, Susie and Alison found themselves in a horrible situation. Anna was more obviously a victim than the other two girls, but all three of them were hurt, physically and emotionally, by the fighting, suspicion and jealousy. All three of them needed to give and receive forgiveness. The girls found that when they forgave each other; they experienced peace, and could become more what God created them to be. In fact, Susie got baptized six months after the end of this story. This forgiveness made a huge difference to their group of friends as well. The animosity between them had started by causing tension within the group, and as it continued, it effectively split the group in two. When Anna, Alison and Susie came to the point of forgiving each other, it healed the rift in the group, as well as healing the three girls as individuals. Through Jesus working in them, the girls could forgive each other and grow closer to God, and the entire group could be united.

We find a similar story when we read John 21. Peter has let Jesus down seriously. With Jesus in his darkest hour, Peter denied he even knew him, not once, but three times: surely a far more hurtful action than a kick or a punch. And the fault is all on Peter's side here. It certainly can't be said that Jesus needed to be forgiven! When we see Peter in this chapter, he is a broken man. Awash with guilt, haunted by his own actions, he retreats and goes back to what he knows best: fishing. Even this doesn't go right. He and his friends fish all night, for nothing. When Jesus appears on the shore, Peter can't wait to see him. He jumps into the sea and swims to the shore, in his hurry. He knows that his only chance to be set free from guilt, move on, and become the man he was created to be, is to be forgiven by Jesus. Confessing sin and receiving forgiveness is fundamental to a relationship with Jesus.[21]

Jesus shows his grace in many ways: by meeting Peter's physical needs with the fish, and then by meeting his emotional and spiritual needs, in forgiving him and commissioning him. Jesus sets Peter free from guilt, and gives him an opportunity to grow closer to him, and become the man he is meant to be. As Bruce Milne observes, 'No matter how desperate our failure, or how deep-seated our shame, [God] can forgive and renew us and then use us in his service. Failure is never final with God.'[22]

We can only guess the impact Peter's failure would have had on the disciples. They would probably have been confused and disheartened by Peter's actions. After all, Jesus had prophesied that Peter would be their leader – the rock on which the church would be built. Could that still be true? They may have been wondering what the future held for them as a group, as well as for Peter as an individual. Jesus responds by bringing the disciples together. He welcomes them all to eat with him, and as he forgives Peter and reinstates him, he reassures the group, unites them and gives them hope for the future.

When my wife and I were making preparations for getting married, we were given a simple and thoroughly biblical piece of advice: 'Don't let the sun go down on your anger' (Ephesians 4:26). It is so much easier to resolve an argument when we are quickly ready to say sorry and forgive each other. A great piece of advice for a marriage. How much more so for a church! Imagine how our churches would be transformed if we all learned to forgive each other!

Think about ...

- Is there someone you know who you need to forgive?
- Is there someone you know who you need to say sorry to?
- How would your church be different if everyone who needed to give or receive forgiveness did so?

A Final Thought...

Young people have so much to offer. They are courageous, passionate, caring and hard working. Young people are doing all kinds of amazing things today in order to share Jesus and change their world and gradually, the world is indeed changing. We have seen so much with our own eyes that convinces us of how valuable young people are, and we hope that we have conveyed that through this book.

This book was designed to share hope. The current generation of young people can bring lasting change to the church, to their communities and to the world. They have the courage, the faith and the creativity to do truly momentous things for the kingdom of God. We are just beginning to see the kind of changes that God can and does bring about through young people. The stories in this book are examples of this. So, there is hope for a bright future, in the church and in the wider world.

There were many other stories that we could

have included in this book. God is already doing so much through young people, and there are countless real-life stories that confirm this. But even bigger and better things could happen in this new generation. If God enables this generation of young people to fulfil their potential, we could see something truly phenomenal happen; something which will transform the world. So, please join with us in praying for young people. Let's pray that the Lord would bless and strengthen this new generation, and work through them to establish his kingdom on earth.

We also urge you to ask yourself what you can do to invest in this generation. How can you support, encourage and build up the young people around you? As you pray for young people, God may reveal more of his plan for them to you. What can you do to be part of this plan and bring it closer to completion?

There is hope for this generation of young people. There is hope for the church and for the world beyond it. Let's pray, dream, invest and see God at work as earth becomes more like heaven and new generations find eternal hope in him.

Notes

1. C. Calver and G. Calver, *On the Front Line*, Oxford: Monarch Books, 2007, p. 53.

2. Article by Jane Shilling, *The Times*, 3 August 2006, p. 8.

3. W. Wiersbe, *The Bible Exposition Commentary*, Wheaton: Victor Books, 1996, John 1:35.

4. B. Milne, *The Message of John: Here Is Your King!*, Leicester: Inter-Varsity Press, 1993, p. 58.

5. B. Milne, *The Message of John: Here Is Your King!*, p. 87.

6. M. Henry, *Matthew Henry's Commentary on the Whole Bible*, Peabody: Hendrickson, 1996, John 2:1.

7. B. Milne, *The Message of John: Here Is Your King!*, p. 63.

8. M. Henry, *Matthew Henry's Commentary on the Whole Bible*, Luke 19.

9. W. Wiersbe, *The Bible Exposition Commentary*, Luke 19.

10. B. Milne, *The Message of John: Here Is Your King!*, p. 138.

11. L. Richards, *The Teacher's Commentary*, Wheaton: Victor Books, 1987, p. 731.

12. J. Walvoord and R. Zuck, *The Bible Knowledge Commentary: An Exposition of the Scriptures*, Wheaton: Victor Books, 1983–c. 1985, p. 320.

13. B. Milne, *The Message of John: Here Is Your King!*,
    p. 196.

14. From The Servant King by Graham Kendrick*

15. L. Richards, *The Teacher's Commentary*, p. 739.

16. J. Stott, *The Message of Acts: The Spirit, the Church &
    the World*, Leicester: Inter-Varsity Press, 1994, p. 34.

17. P. Brierley, *Reaching and Keeping Tweenagers*,
    London: Christian Research, 2002, p. 129.

18. K. Chafin and L. Ogilvie, *The Preacher's Commentary
    Series, Volume 30: 1, 2 Corinthians*, Nashville:
    Thomas Nelson Inc., 1985, p. 219.

19. W. Wiersbe, *The Bible Exposition Commentary*, Luke
    24:13.

20. W. Wiersbe, *The Bible Exposition Commentary*, Luke
    14:25.

21. B. Milne, *The Message of John: Here Is Your King!*,
    p. 317.

22. B. Milne, *The Message of John: Here Is Your King!*,
    p. 317.

FREEDOM IN CHRIST
FOR YOUNG PEOPLE   A 13-SESSION
DISCIPLESHIP COURSE

Growing as a Christian is a process of exploring and finding out more about Jesus and more about the person that He created each of us to be. The Freedom in Christ course is specifically designed to help young people grow in faith and maturity.

The aim of *Freedom in Christ for Young People* is to set young people firmly on the way to becoming disciples of Jesus who are sold out for him and will make a radical difference in the world in which they live. Watch them change as they connect with the truth about who they are in Christ, become free from pressures that hold them back and learn to renew their thinking – no matter what their circumstances or background.

Whilst the world of young people tells them that they have to look a certain way or achieve to be loved and fit in, this course will help them discover the truth through the power of God's Word leading to a powerful, life-changing experience. Finding freedom from these lies and the stuff that holds them back has the potential not only to transform the young person themselves but also the world around them.

The course is based on the hugely successful *Freedom In Christ Discipleship Course* (over 100,000 users in the UK) and can be run alongside the adult course in your church. This young people's version contains relevant, interactive, multi-media based material tailored to meet the needs of 11-18 year olds. It's packed full of age-appropriate games, activities, discussion-starters, film clip suggestions and talk slots, all provided in the Leader's Guide.

"Every young disciple is looking to engage with Jesus in a way that will change lives. This innovative, exciting course will help young people discover the truth of who they are in Christ and set them free to be all that God has made them as a result. "

- Mike Pilavachi, founder and director of Soul Survivor

"Freedom in Christ is a creative and relevant course for teenagers with the potential to produce a generation of fruitful young disciples."

- Martin Saunders, editor of Youthwork Magazine

The materials come in three parts:

LEADER'S GUIDE

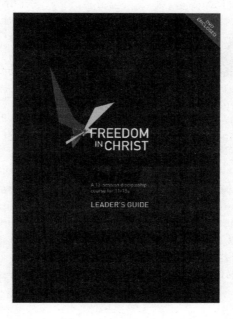

This is the full Leader's Guide for the course, comprising the complete text for all 13 weeks for both age streams; 11-14 and 15-18. The youth version of the 'Steps to Freedom in Christ' weekend is also included, along with a DVD containing approximately two hours of related training material.

The book includes introduction, leader's notes, an outline programme and planning tools, plus the leader's training DVD. Price includes VAT.

ISBN 978-1-85424-923-4, £30.00

WORKBOOK FOR 11-14S

The workbook contains summaries of all key points with well-thought-out questions to help participants get the most from the course. There is space in the text for course members to enter their personal responses and make the workbook their own. The workbook covers the 'Steps to Freedom in Christ' weekend.

ISBN 978-1-85424-924-1, single copy, £2.99
ISBN 978-1-85424-925-8, pack of five, £12.99

WORKBOOK FOR 15-18S

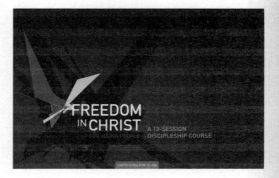

The equivalent workbook for older teens, with material and questions tailored to this age group.

ISBN 978-1-85424-926-5, single copy, £2.99
ISBN 978-1-85424-927-2, pack of five, £12.99

All materials can be ordered from your local Christian bookshop, or from British Youth for Christ (www.yfc.co.uk) or from Freedom in Christ (www.ficm.org.uk).

Published by Monarch Books in conjunction with Freedom in Christ and Youth for Christ.